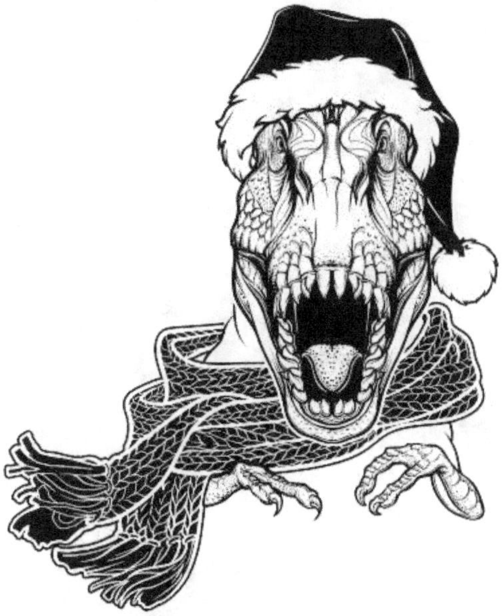

This Stoners Psychedelic Coloring Book

-Belongs To-

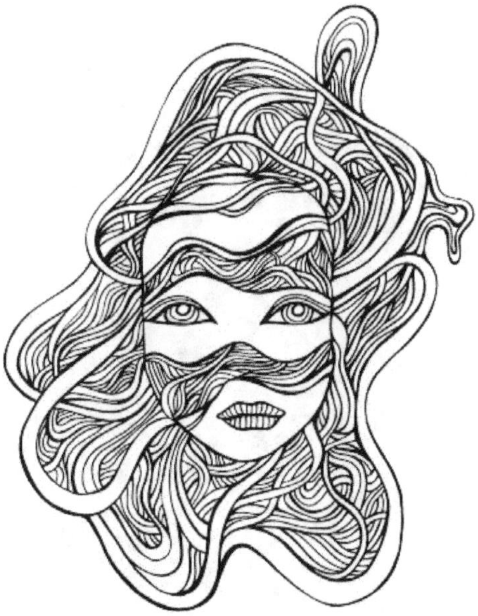

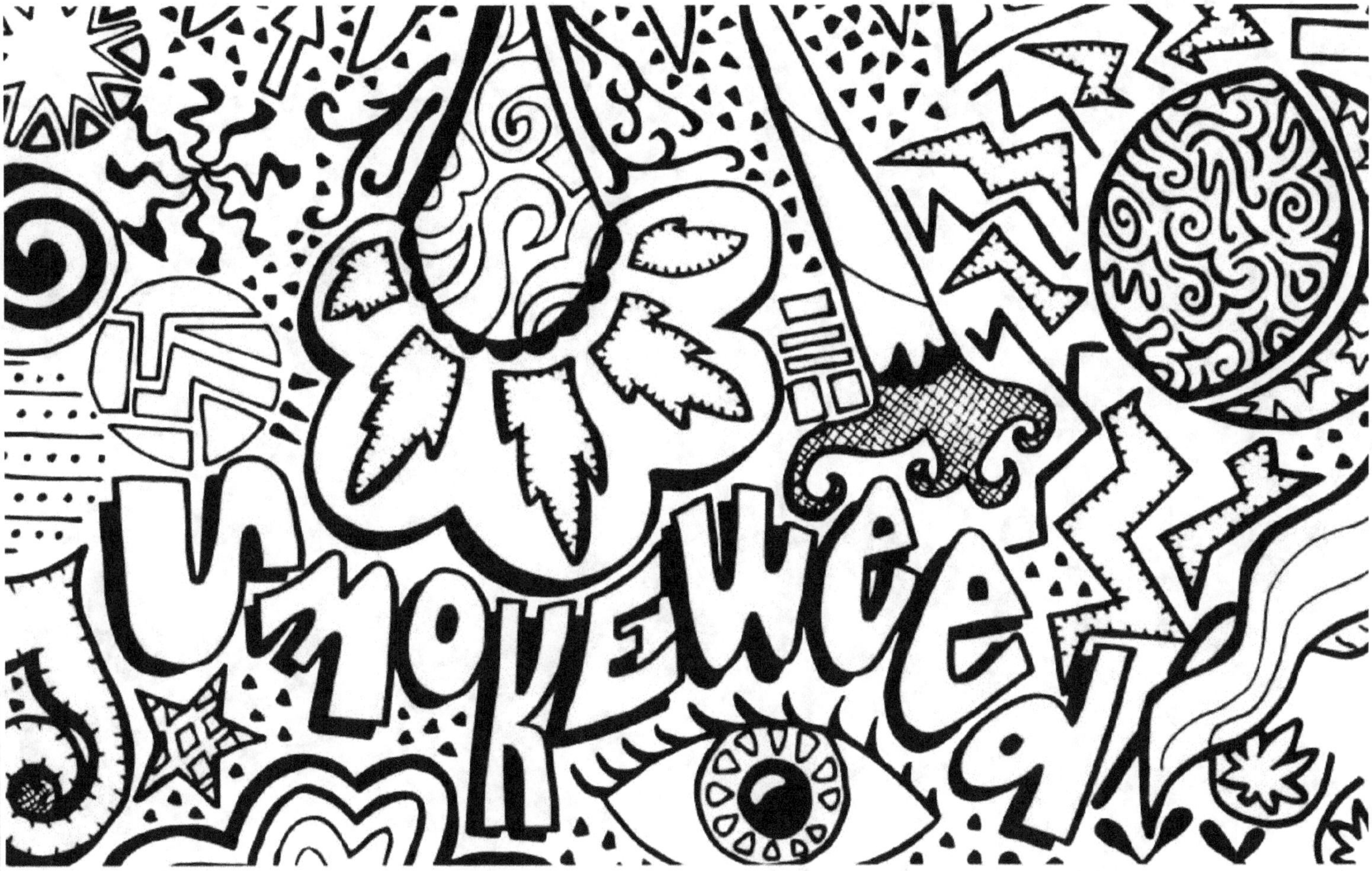
Smokeweed!

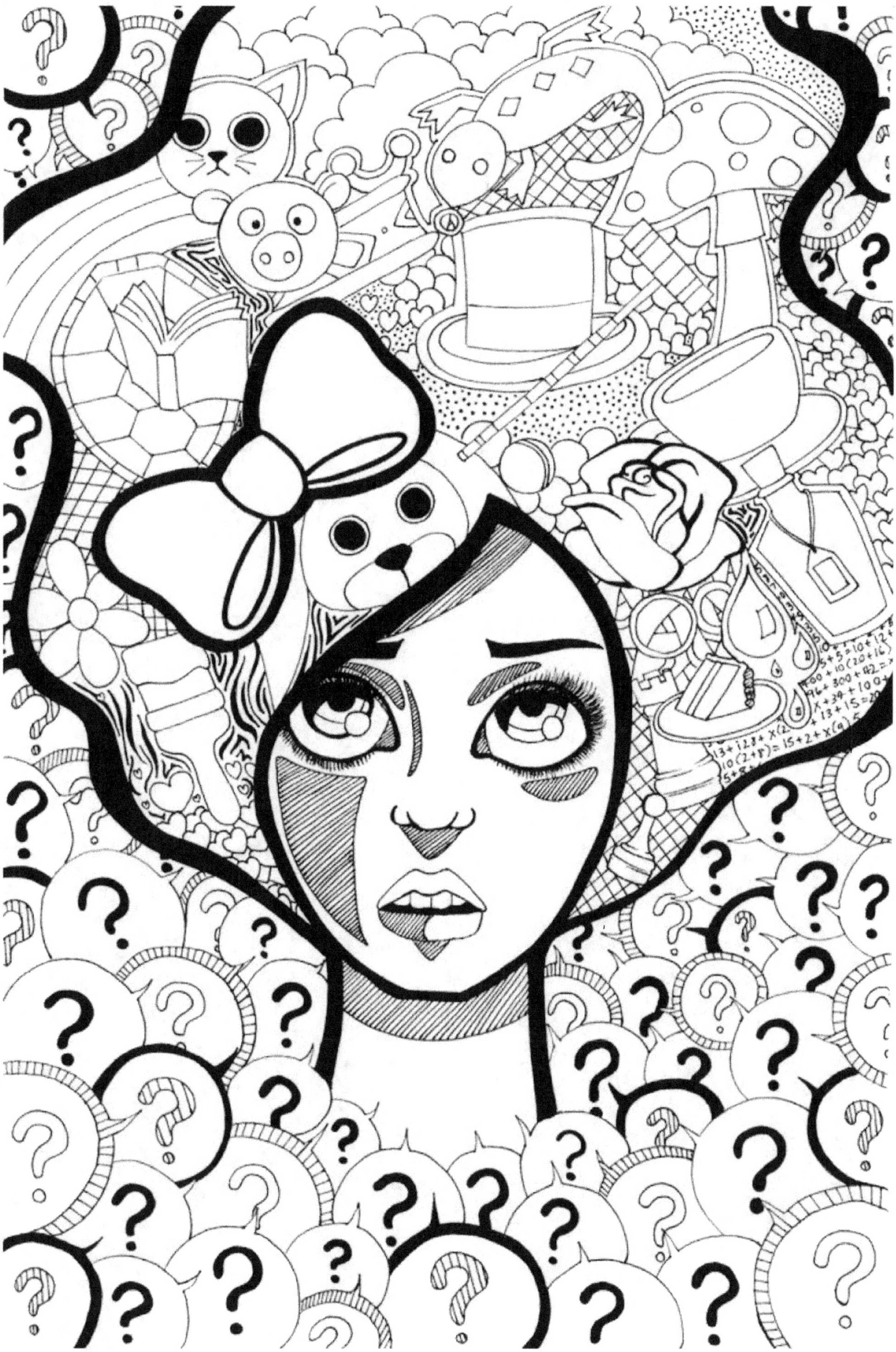

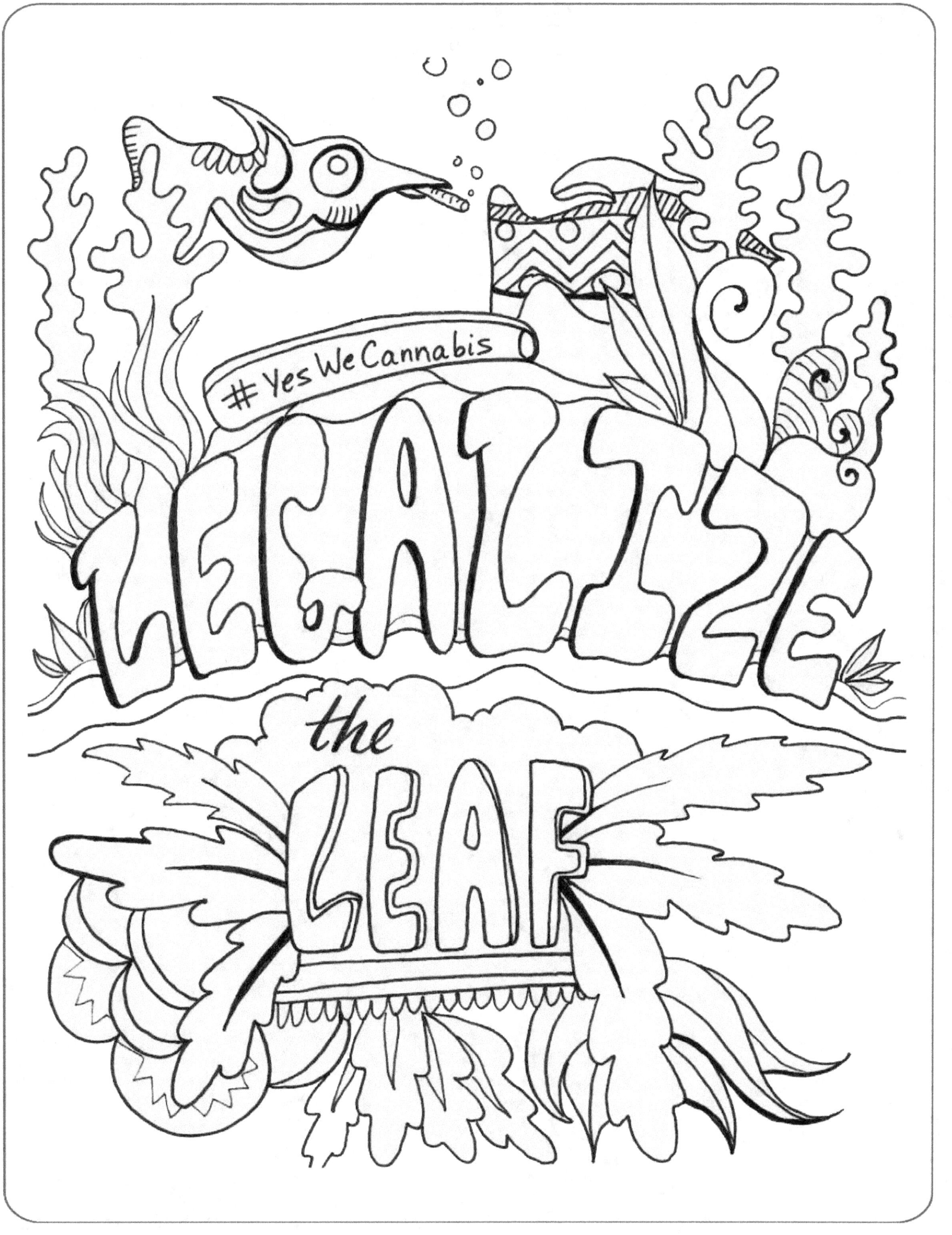
#YesWeCannabis
LEGALIZE
the
LEAF

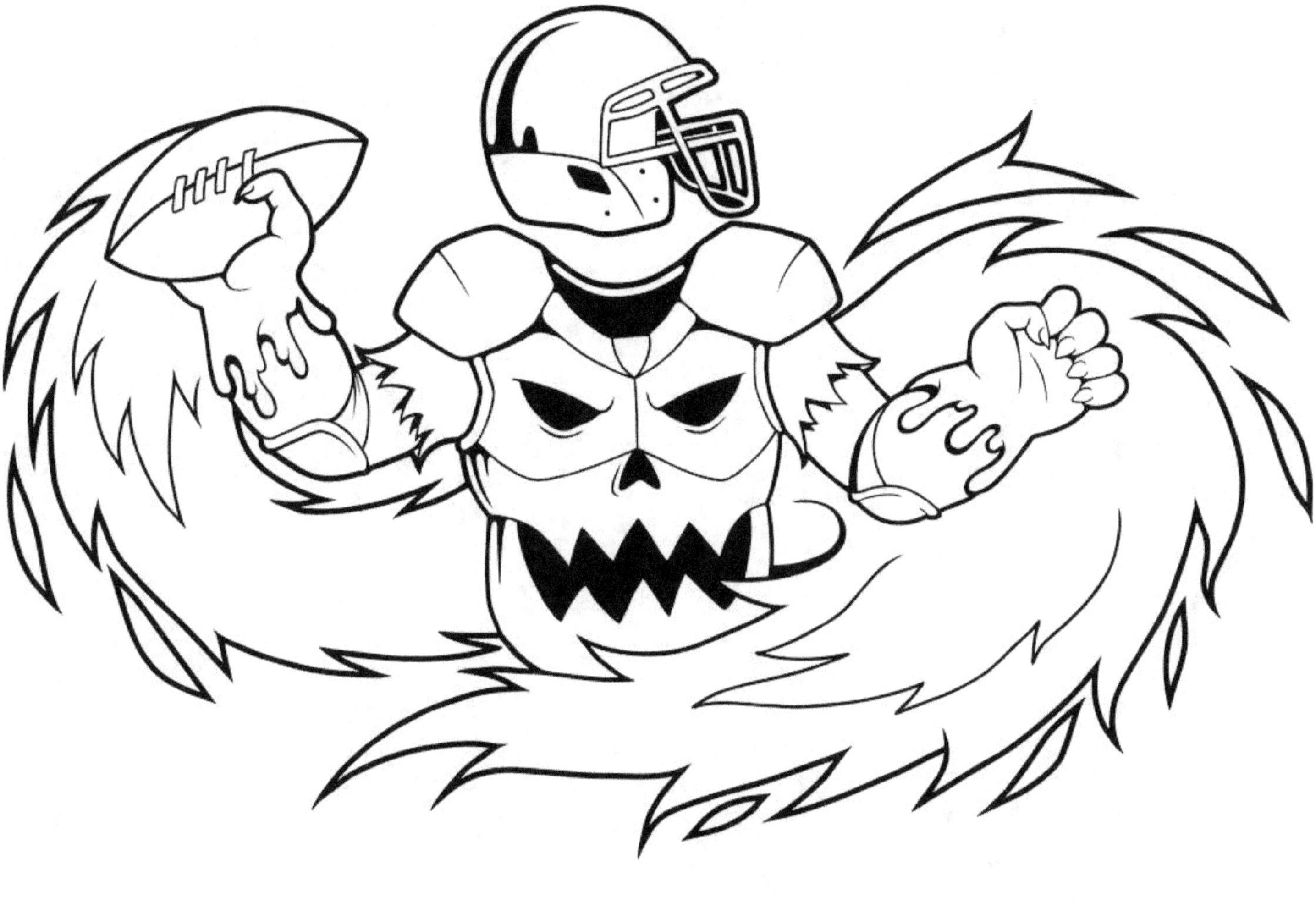

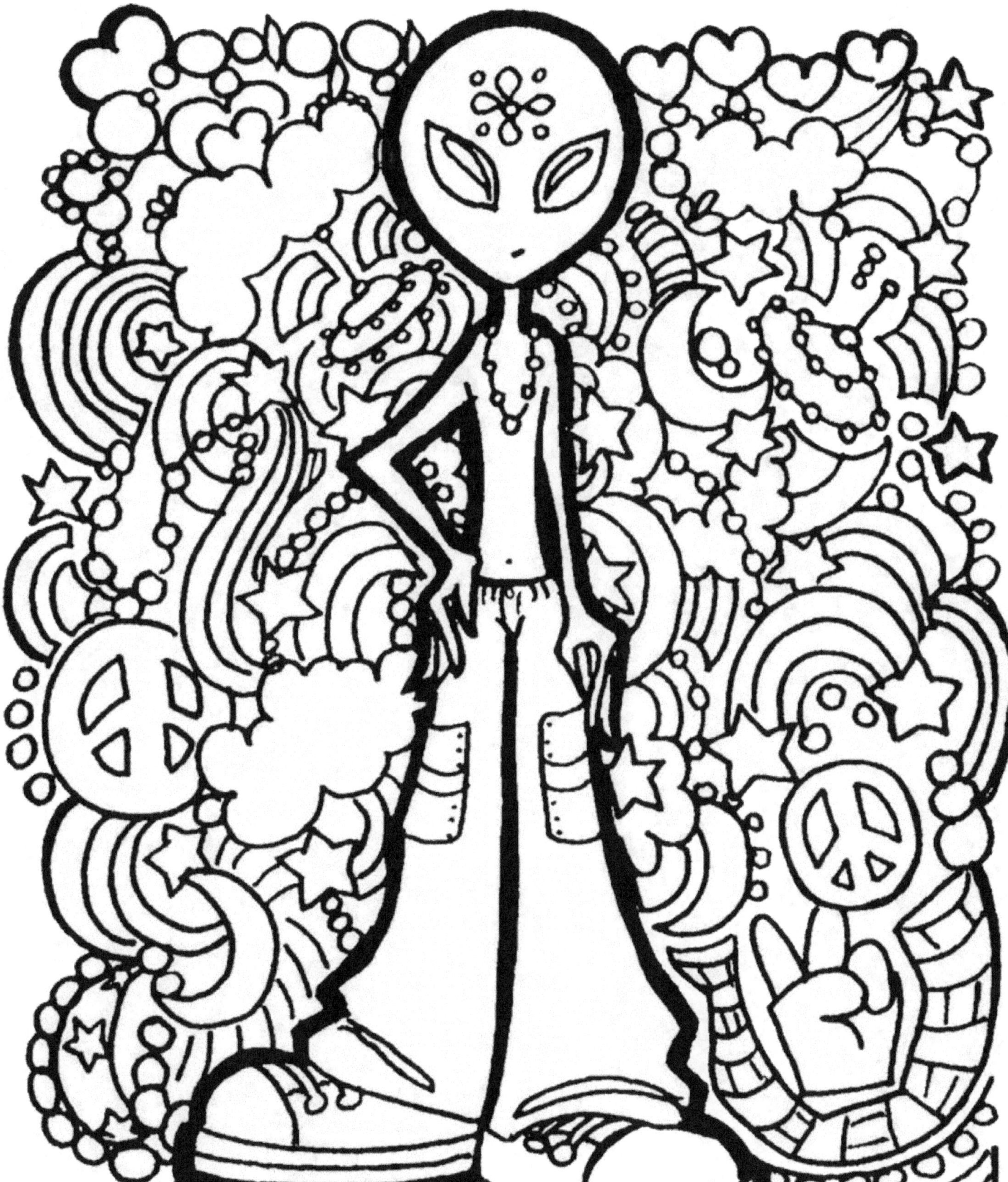

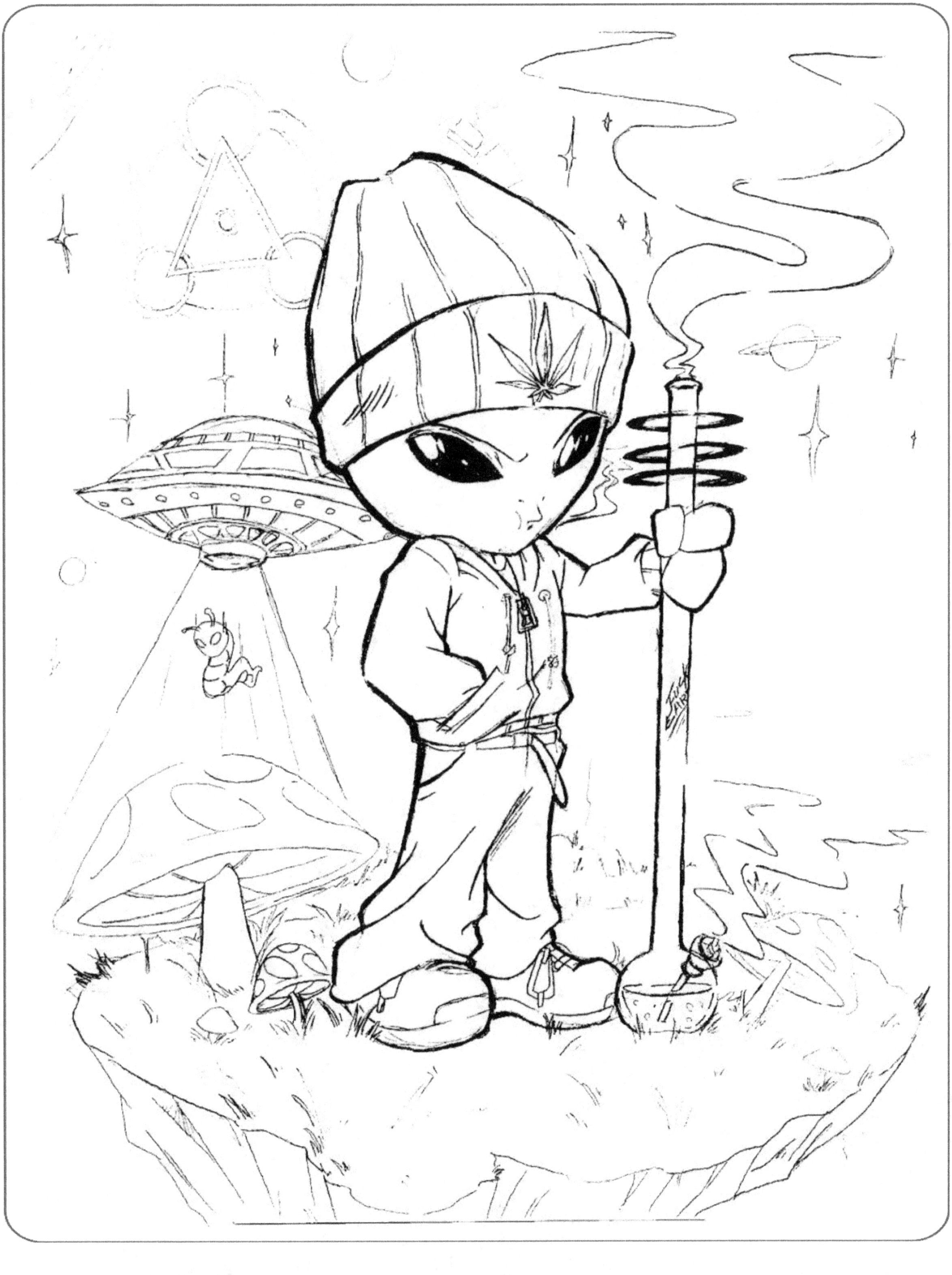

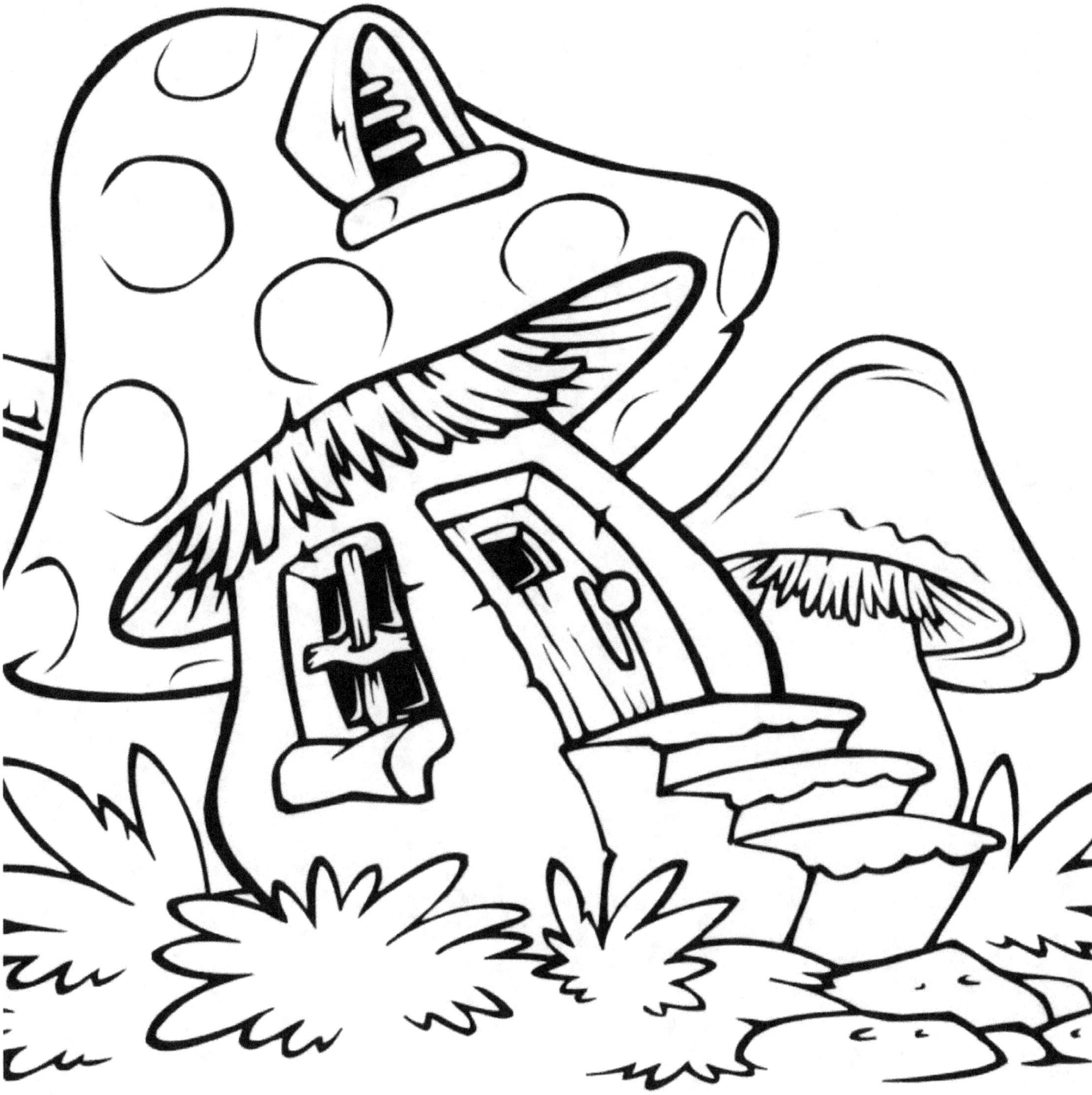

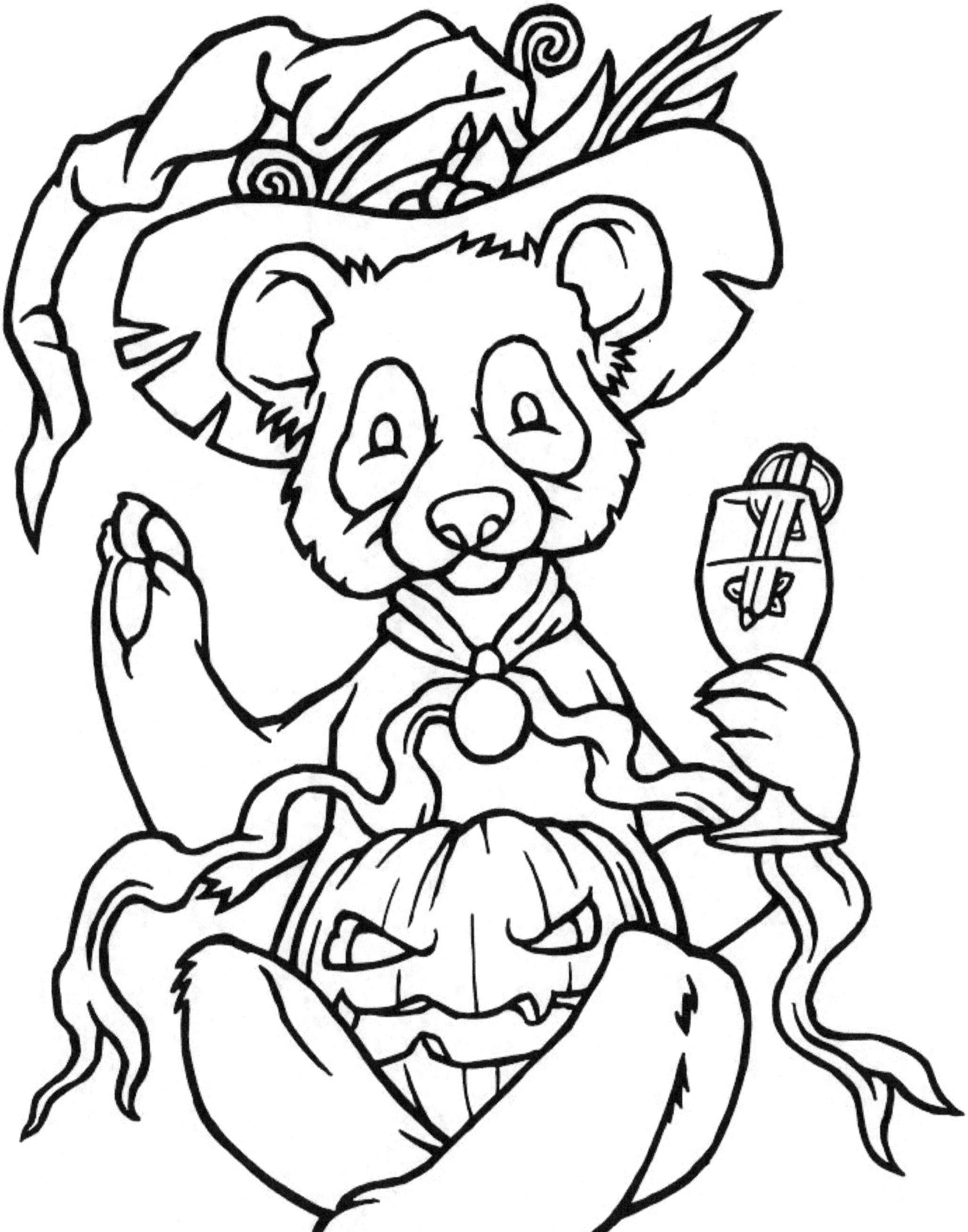

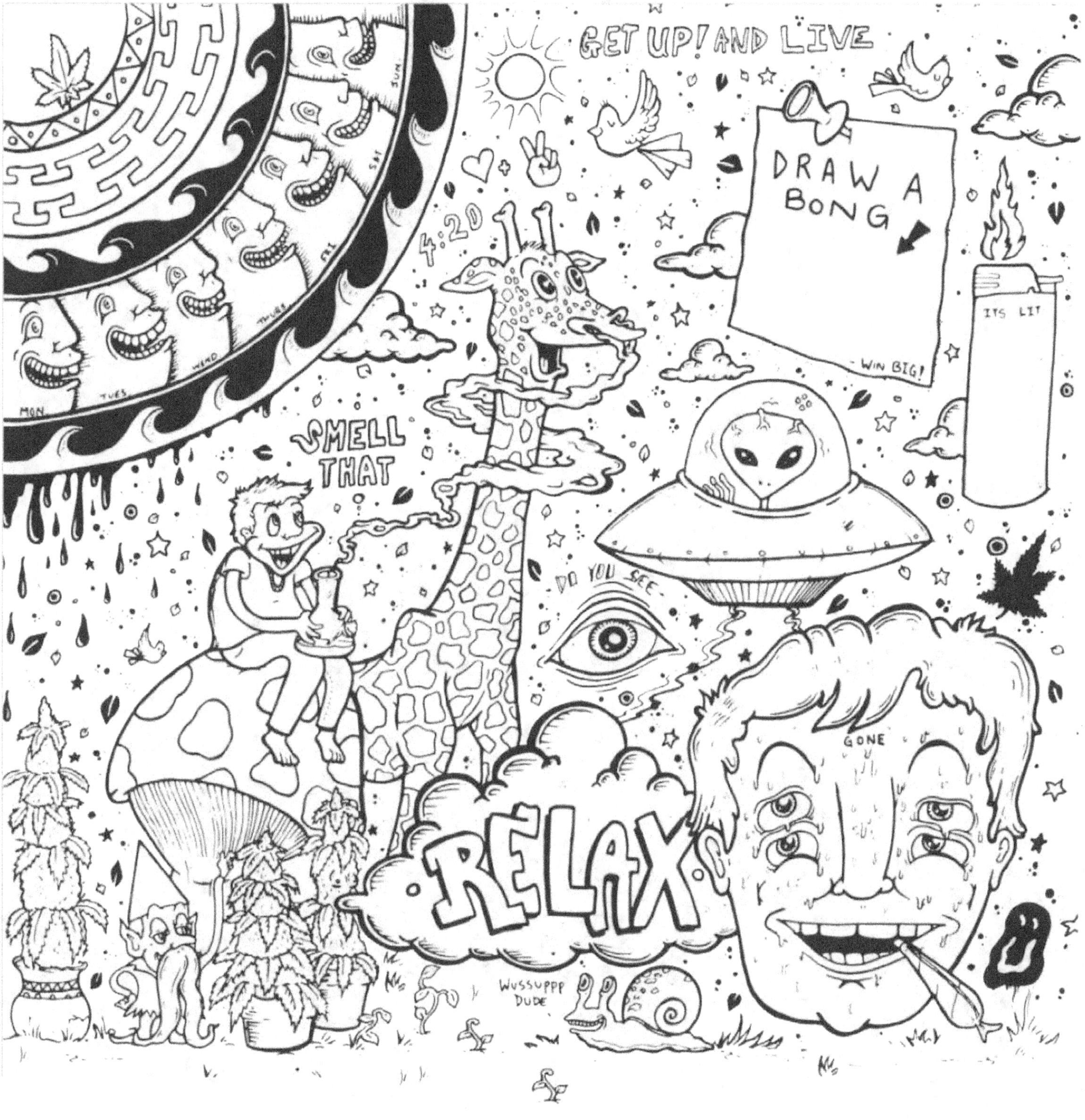
GET UP! AND LIVE
DRAW A BONG
WIN BIG!
ITS LIT
4:20
SMELL THAT
DO YOU SEE
RELAX
GONE

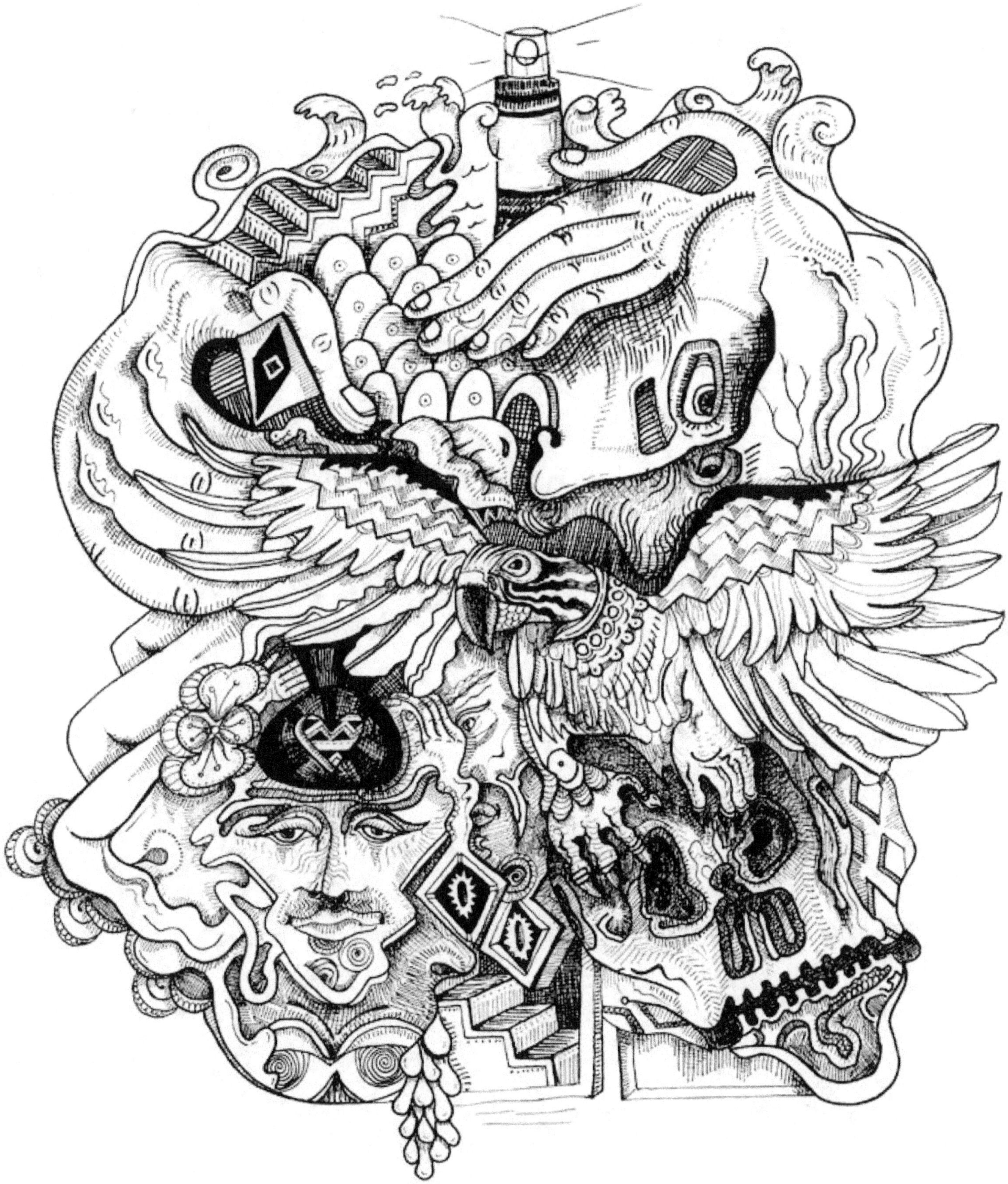

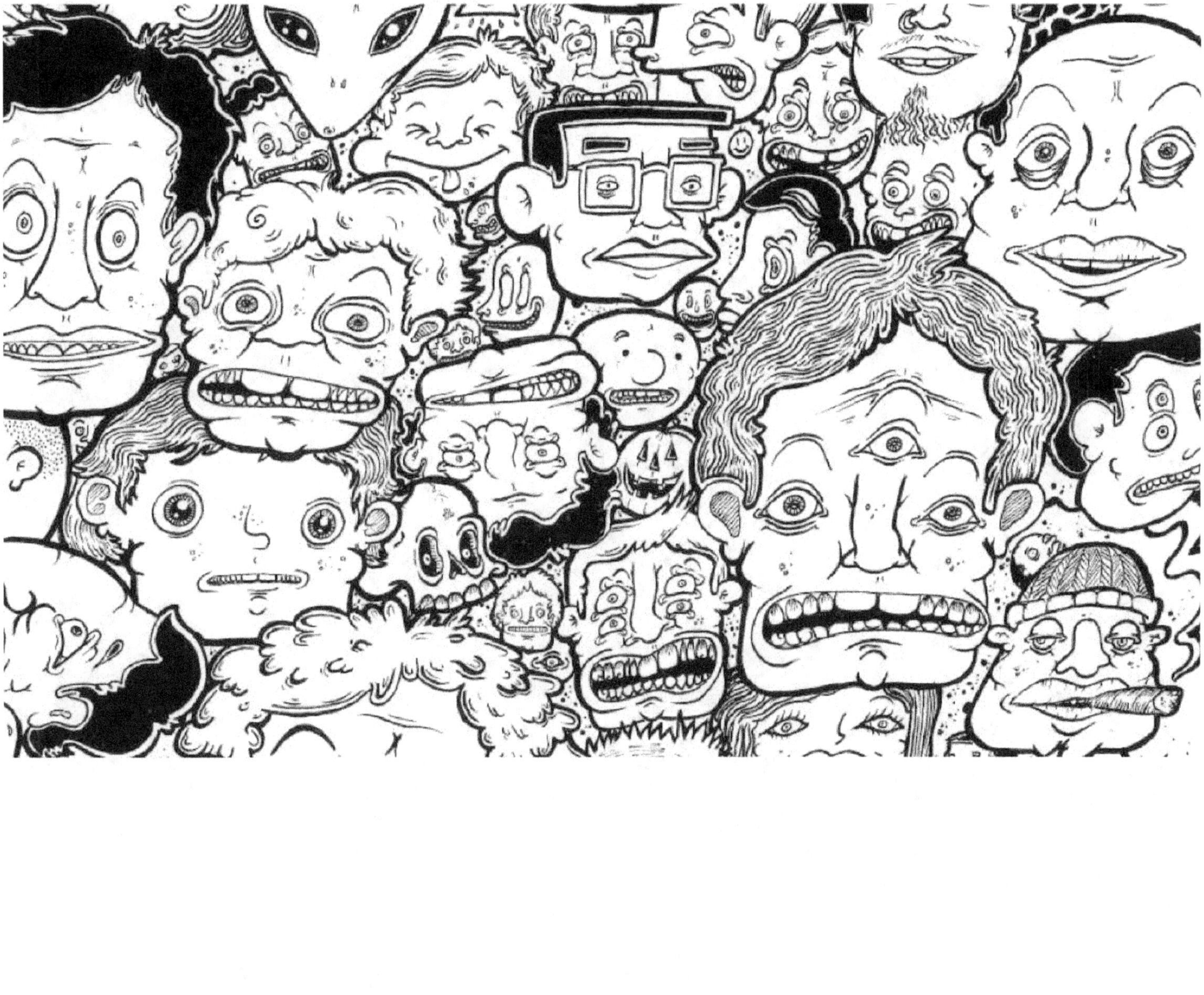

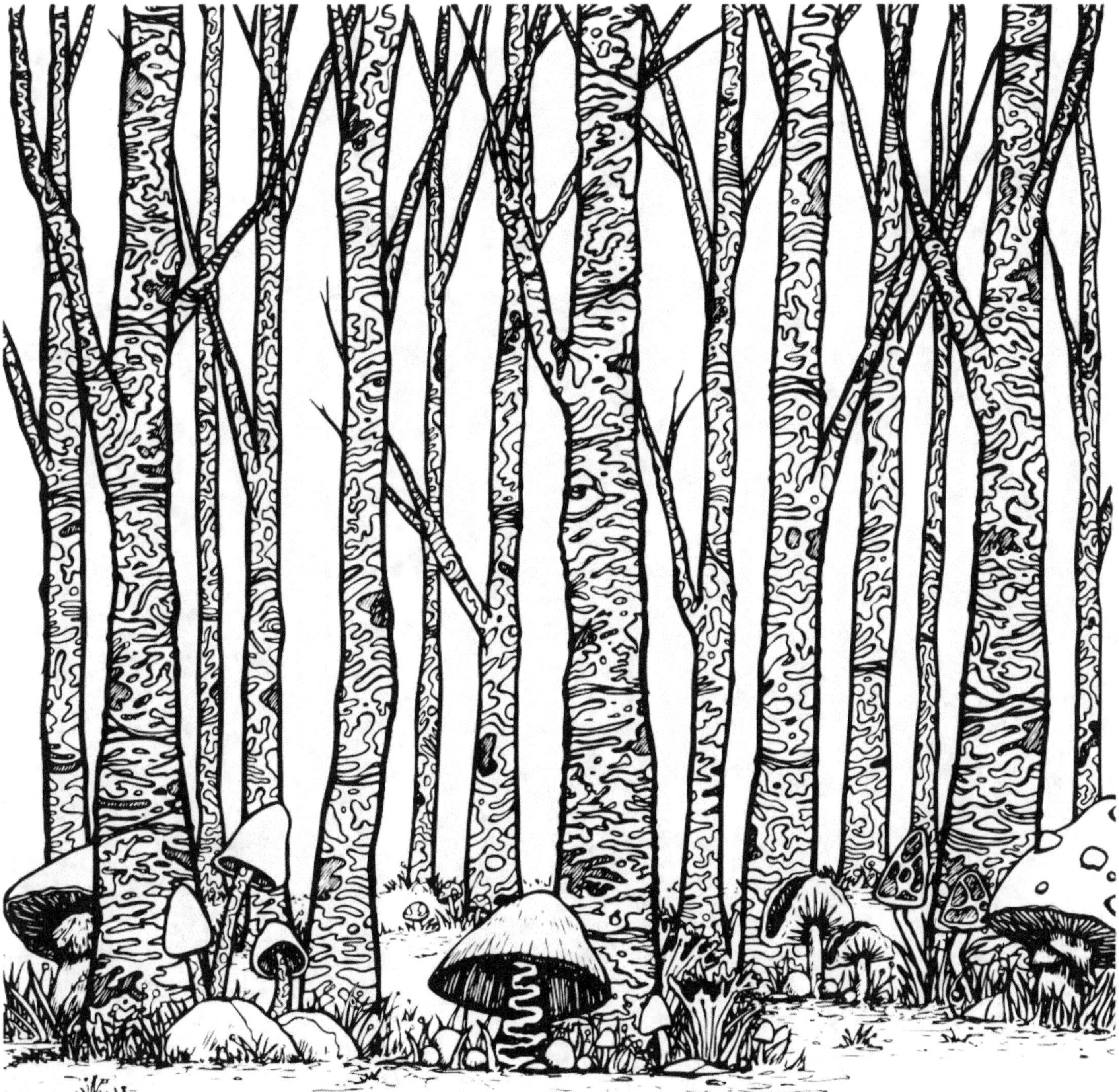

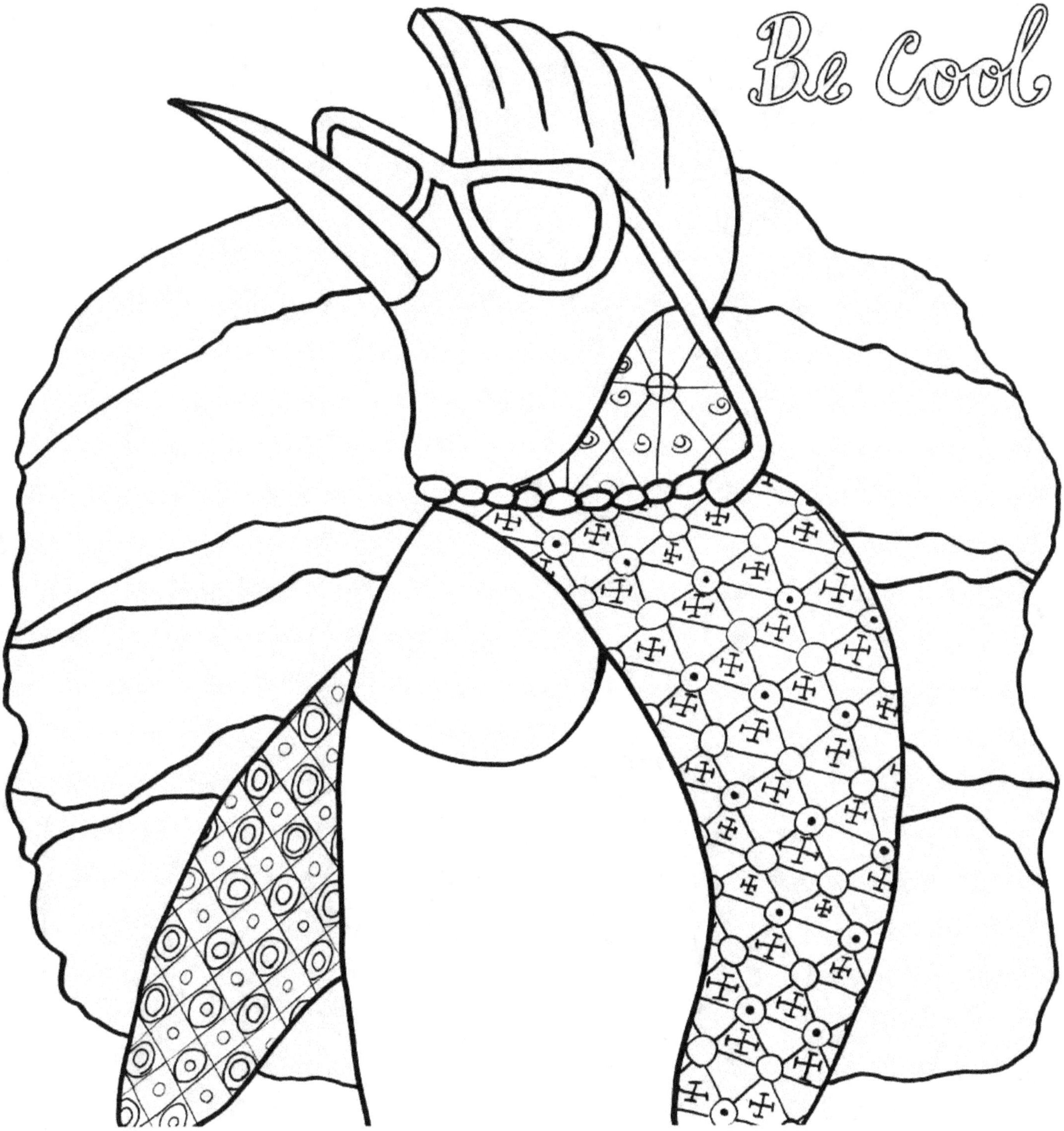
Be Cool

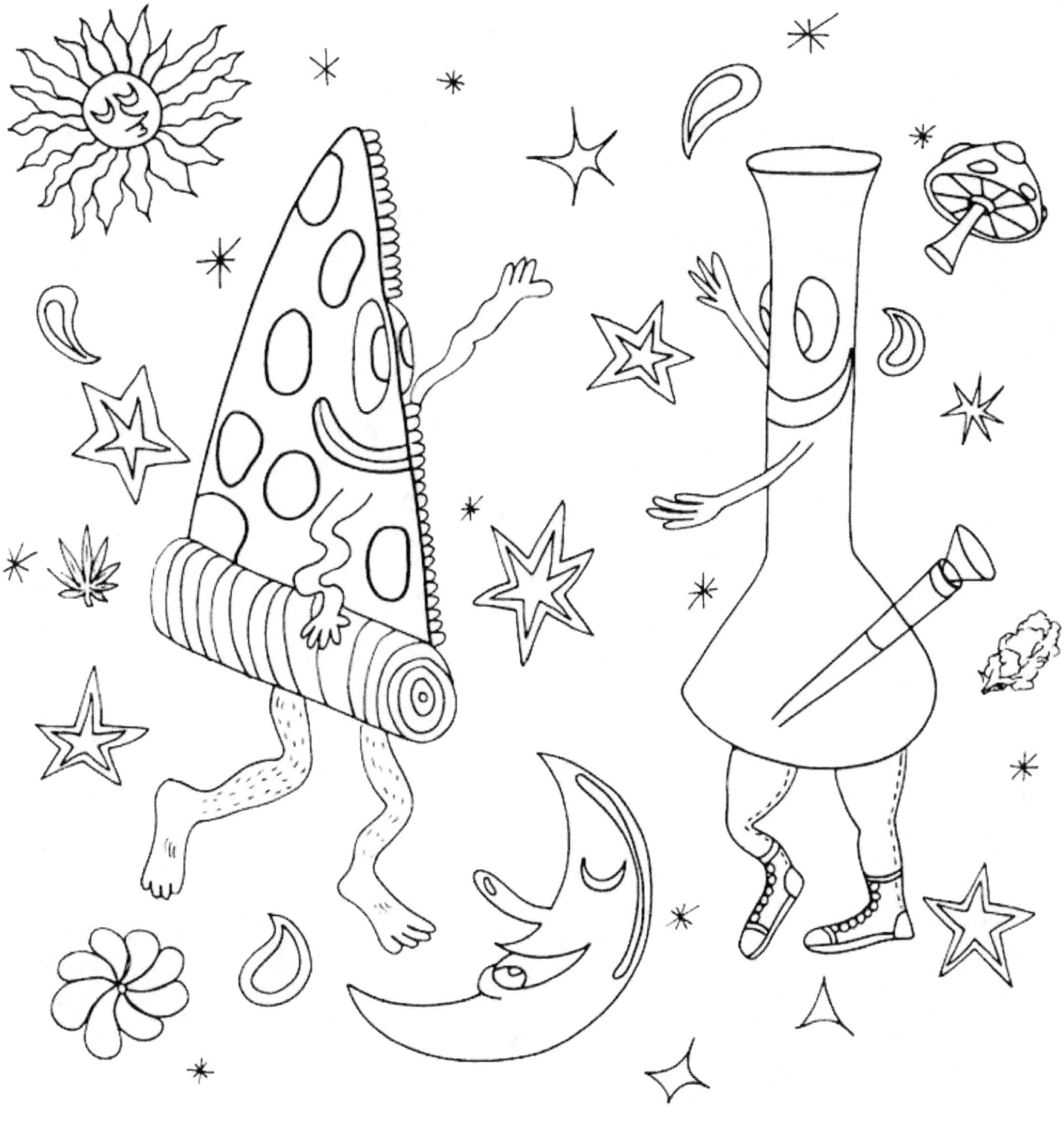

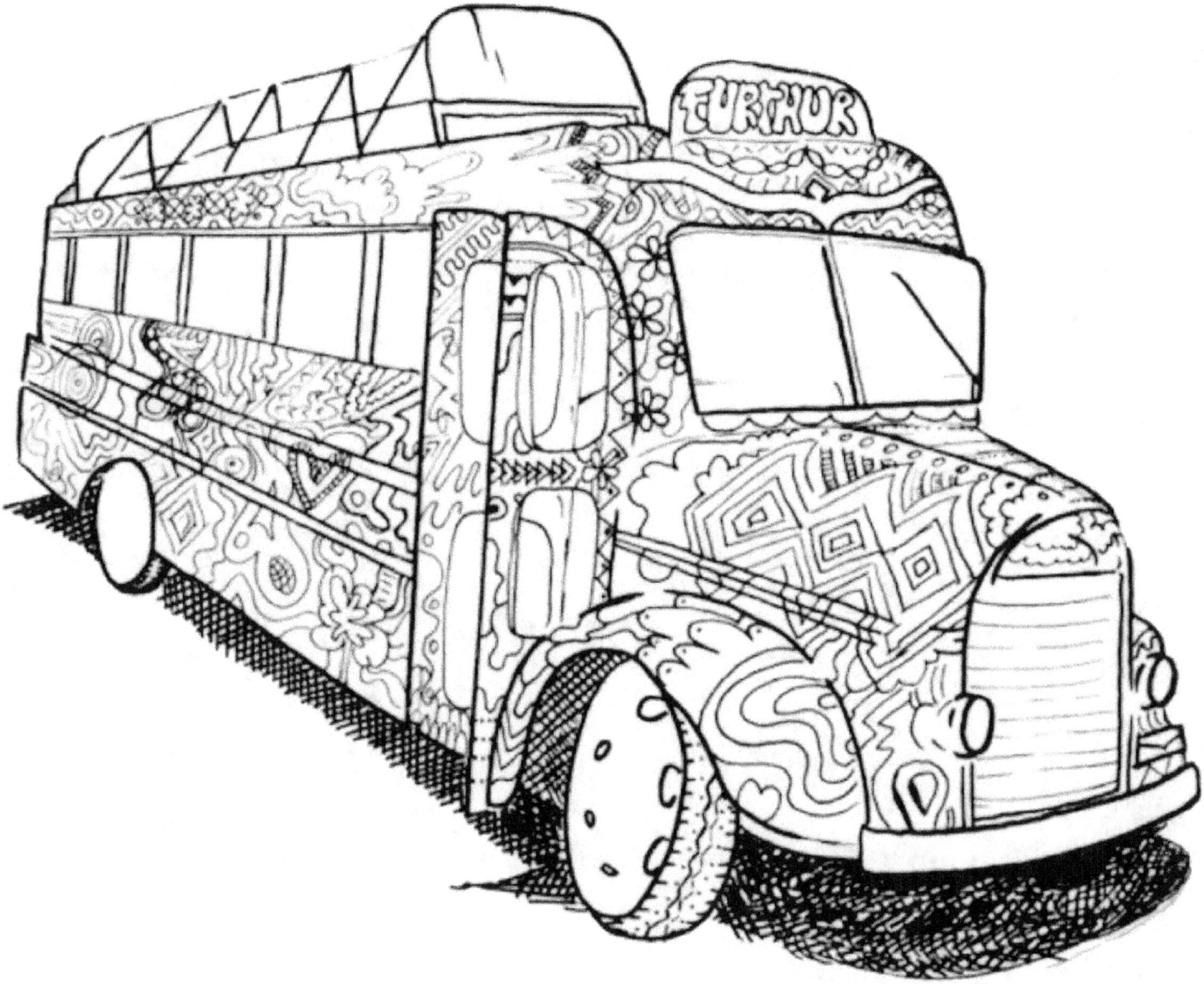
FURTHUR

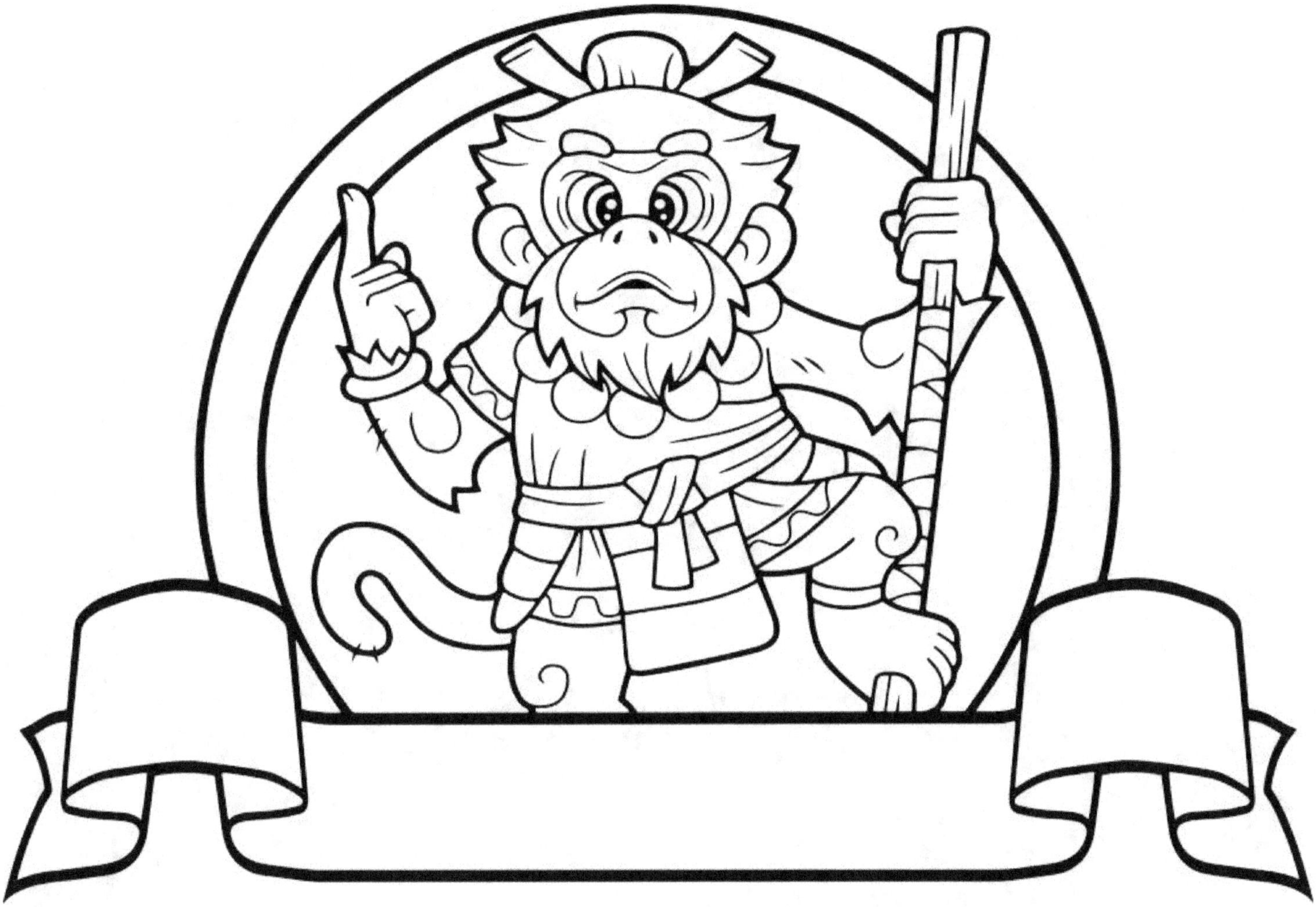

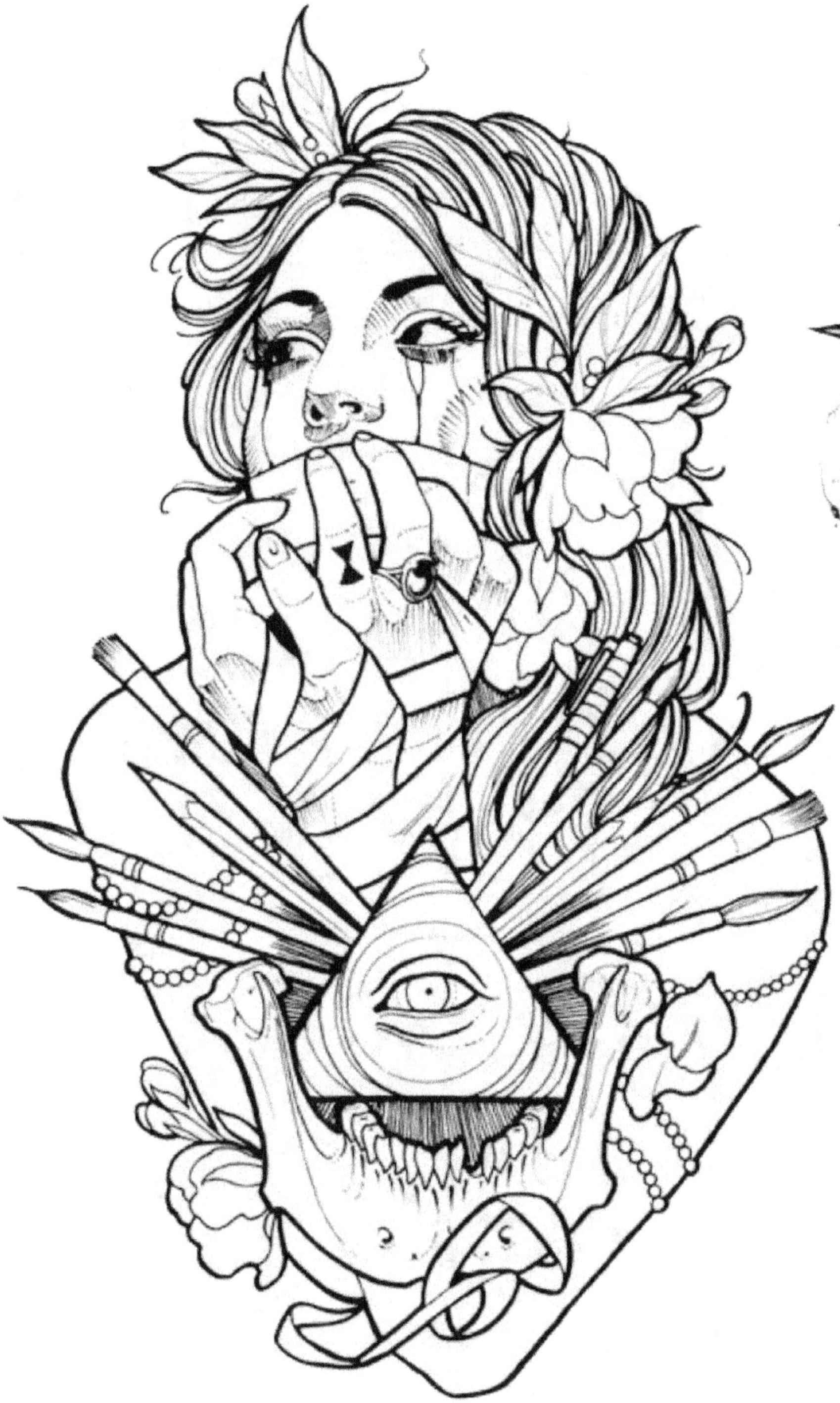

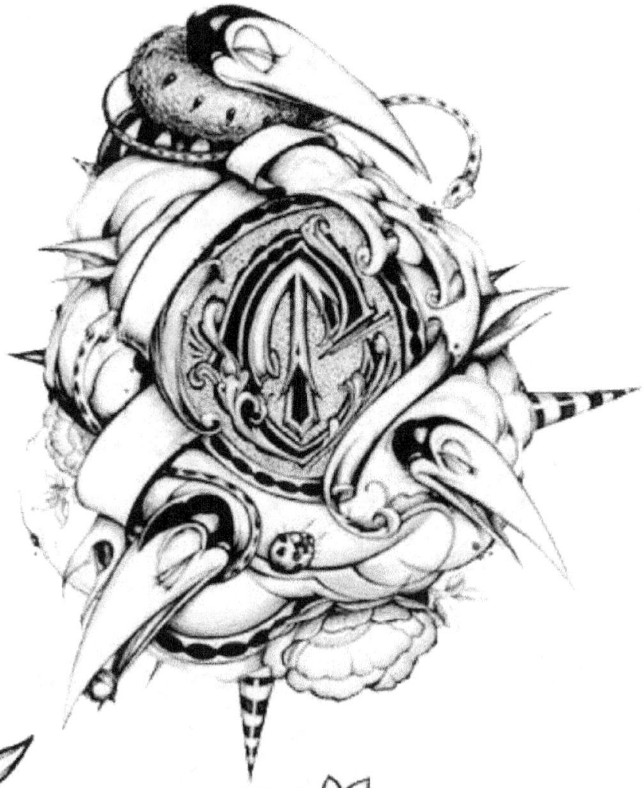

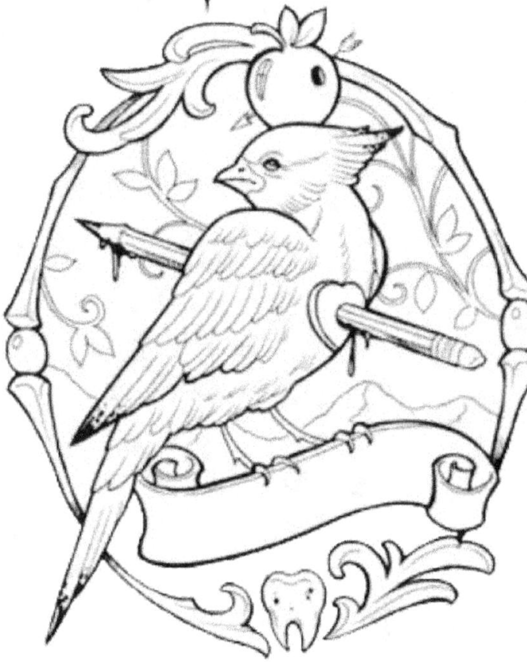

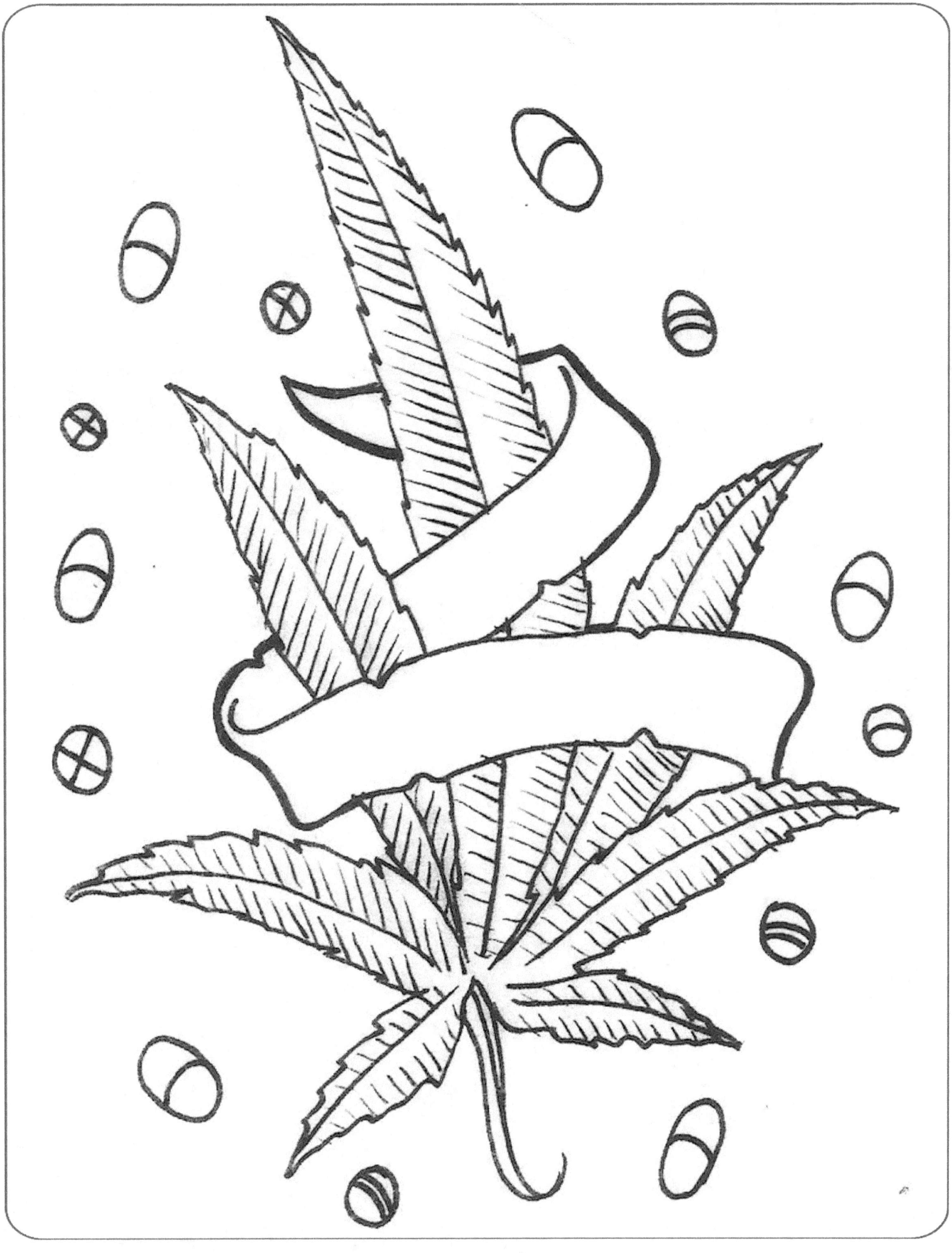

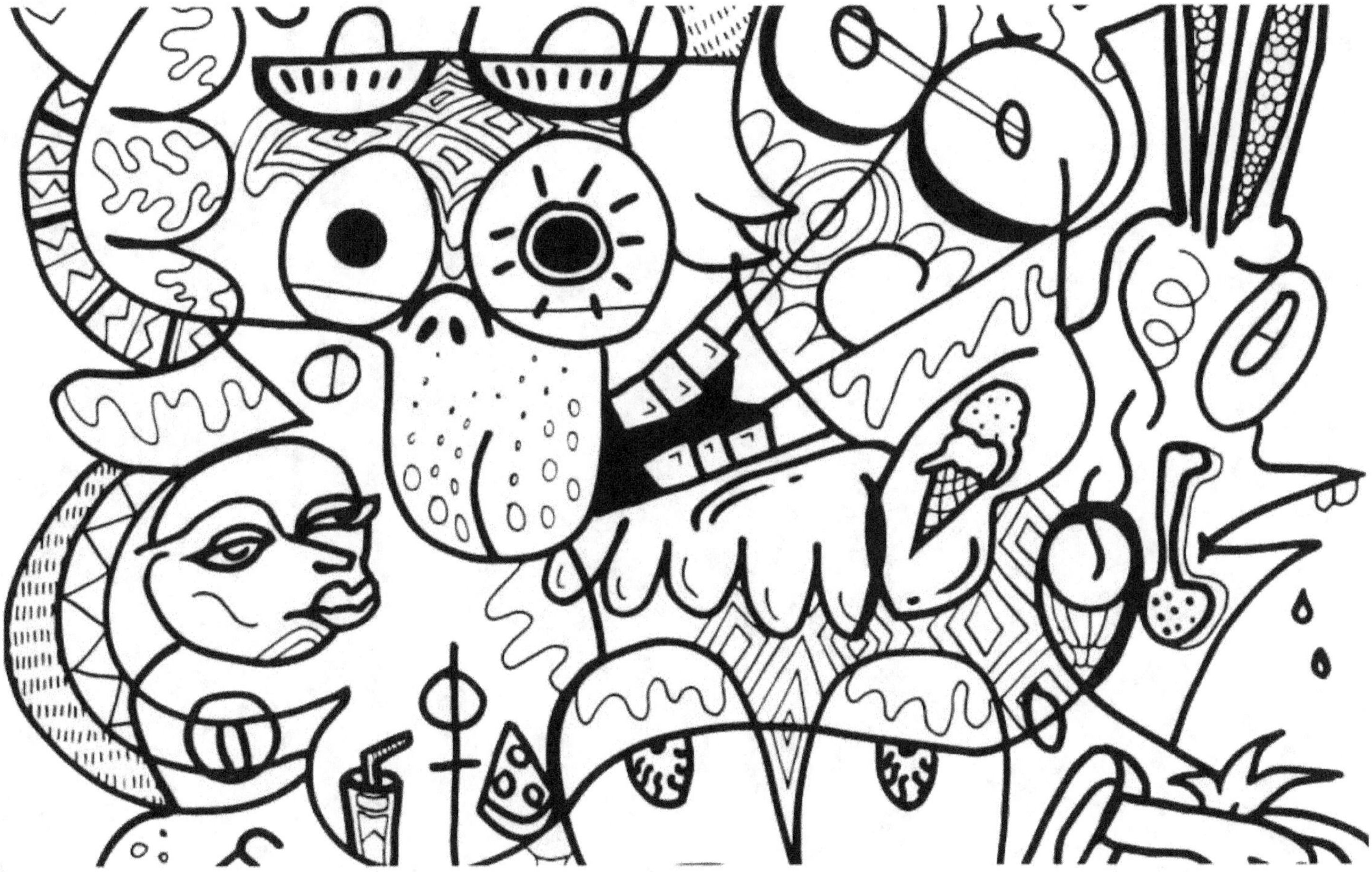

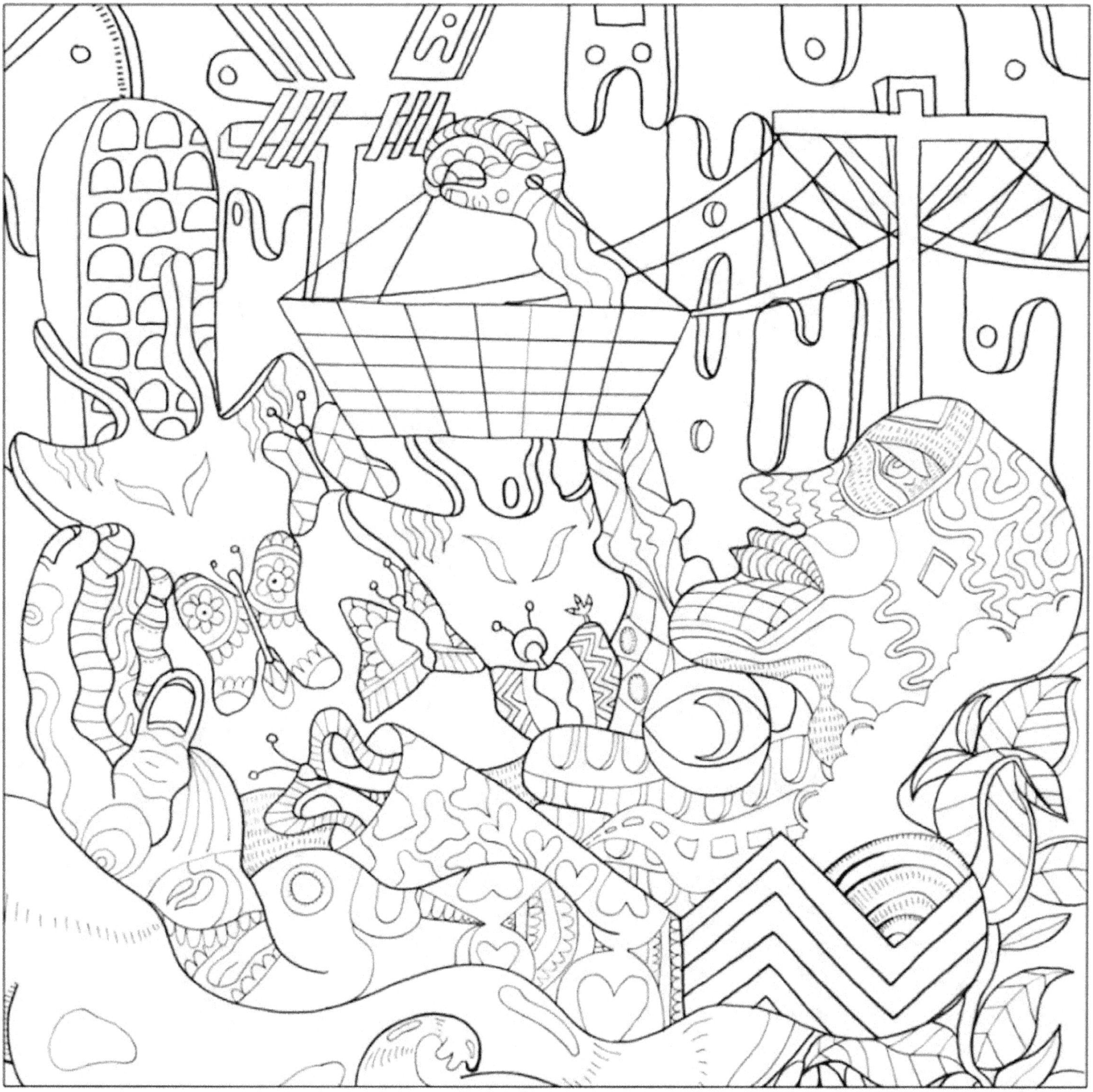

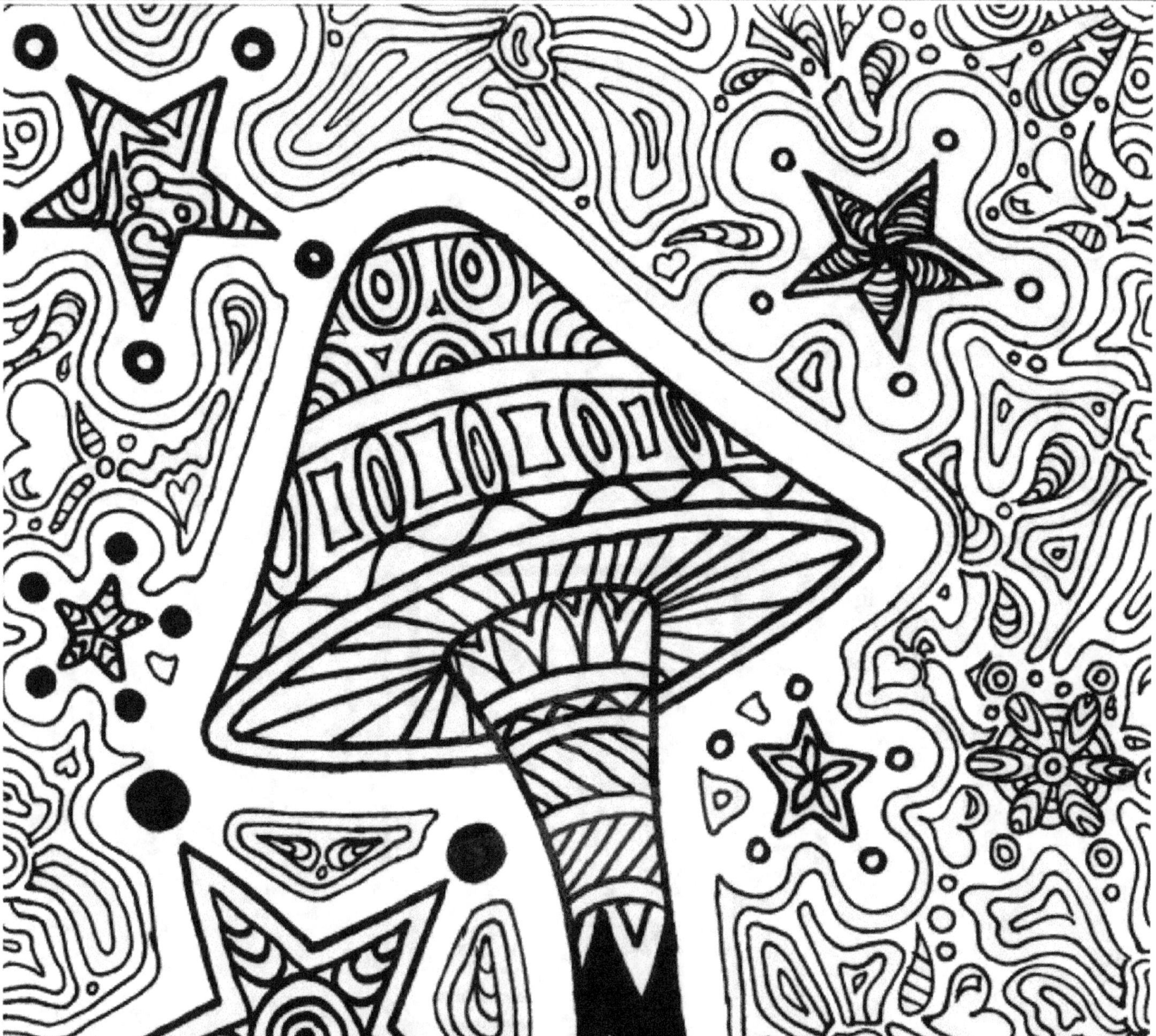
-FAIRY '03

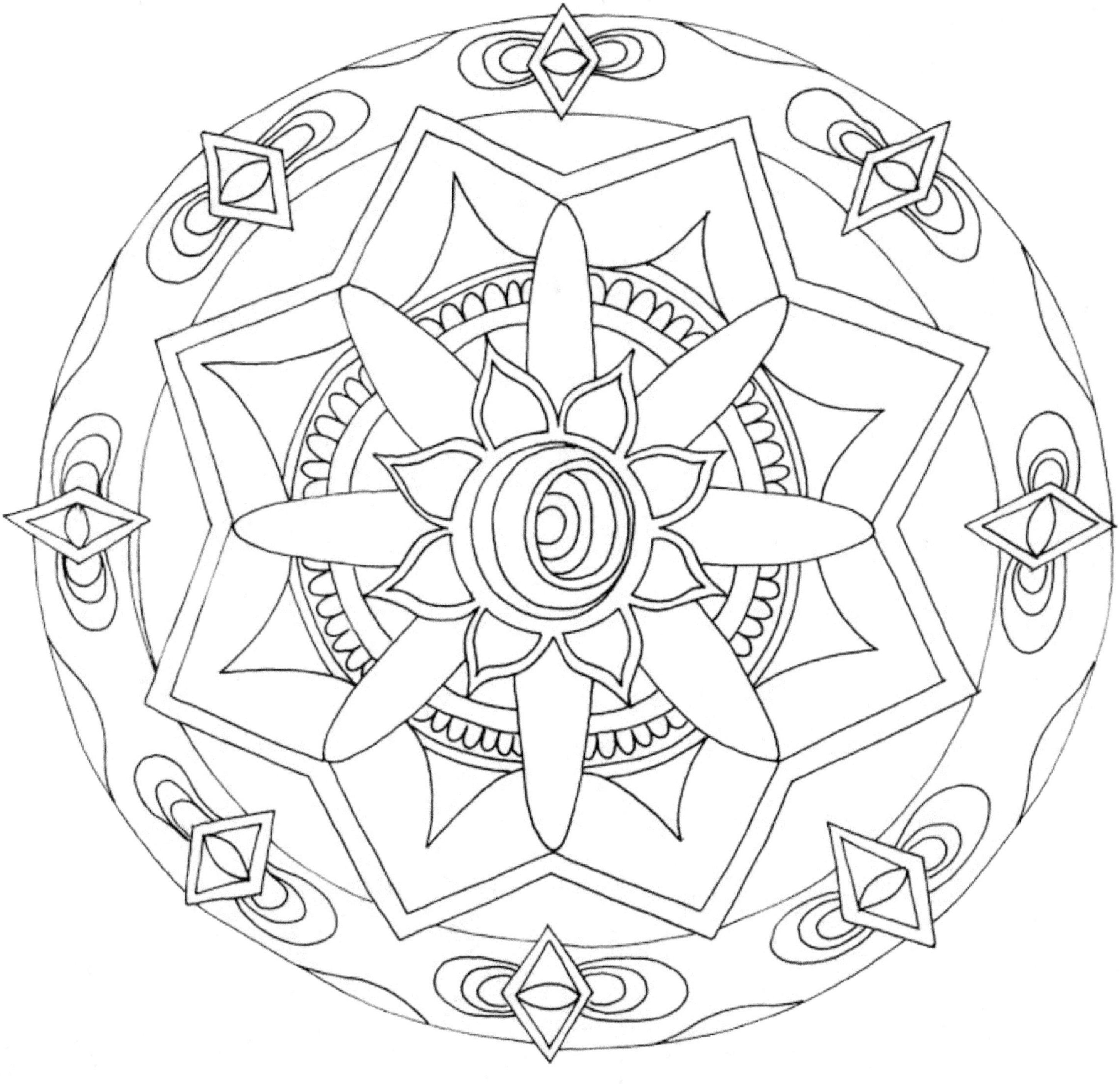

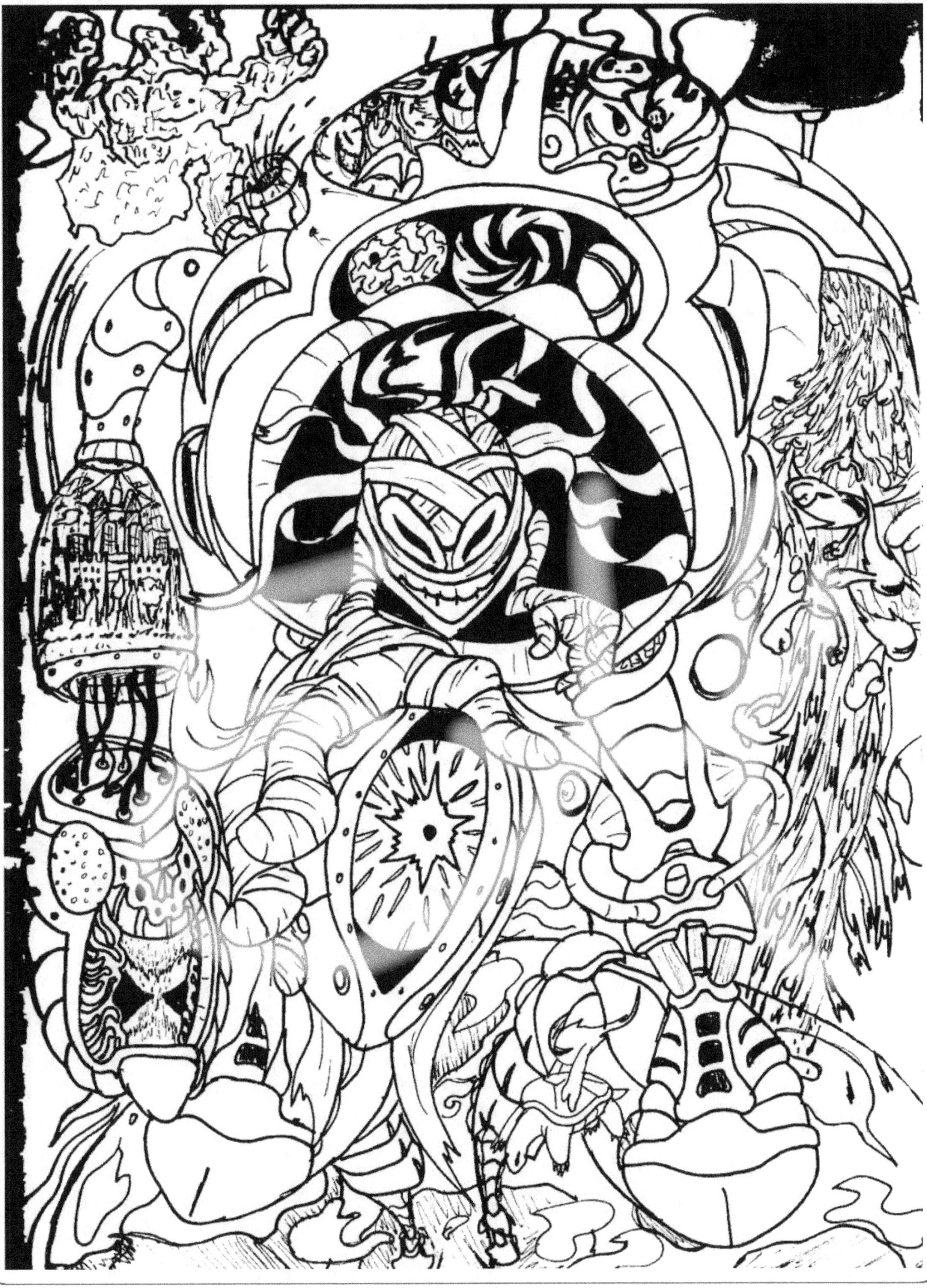

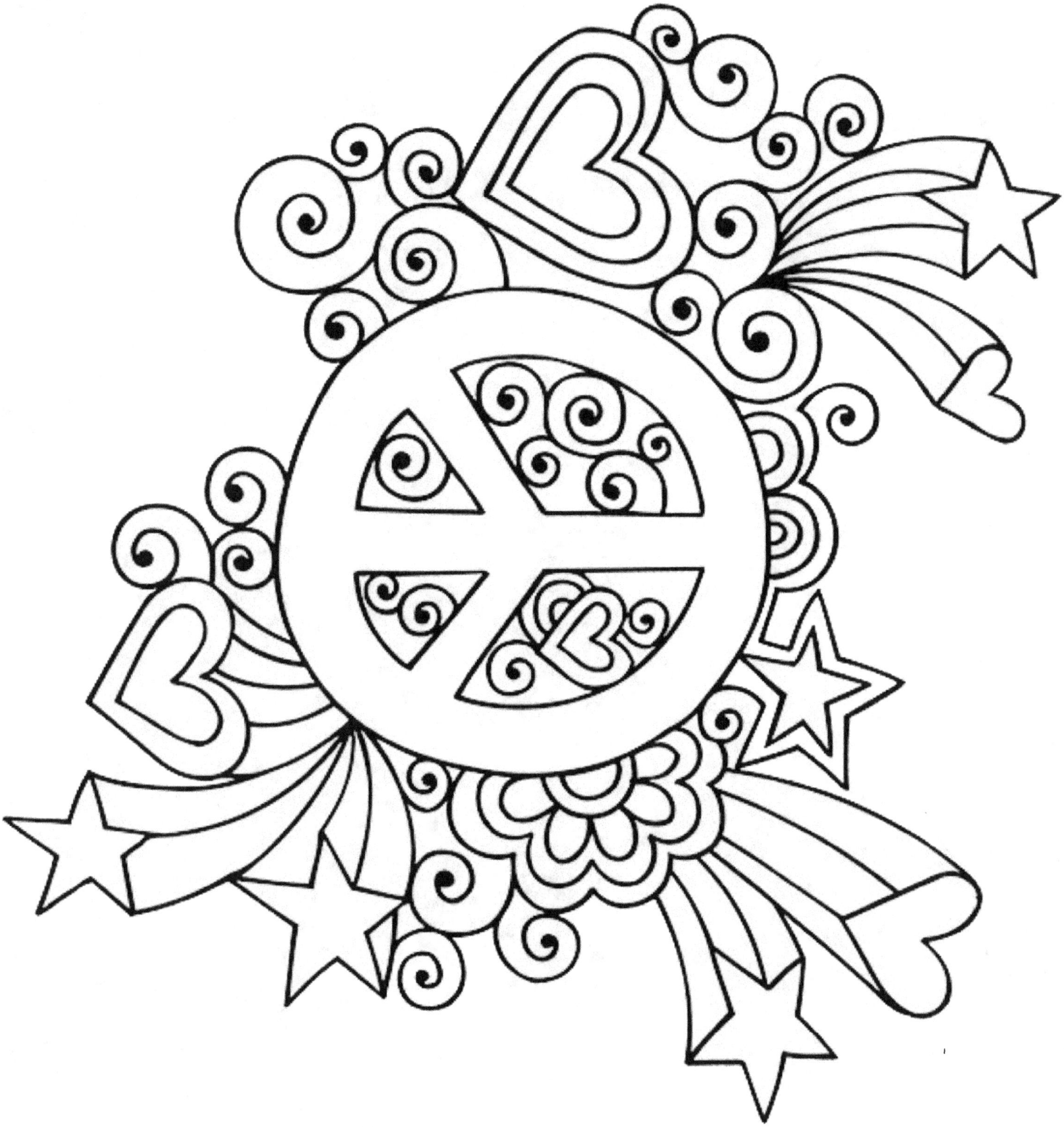

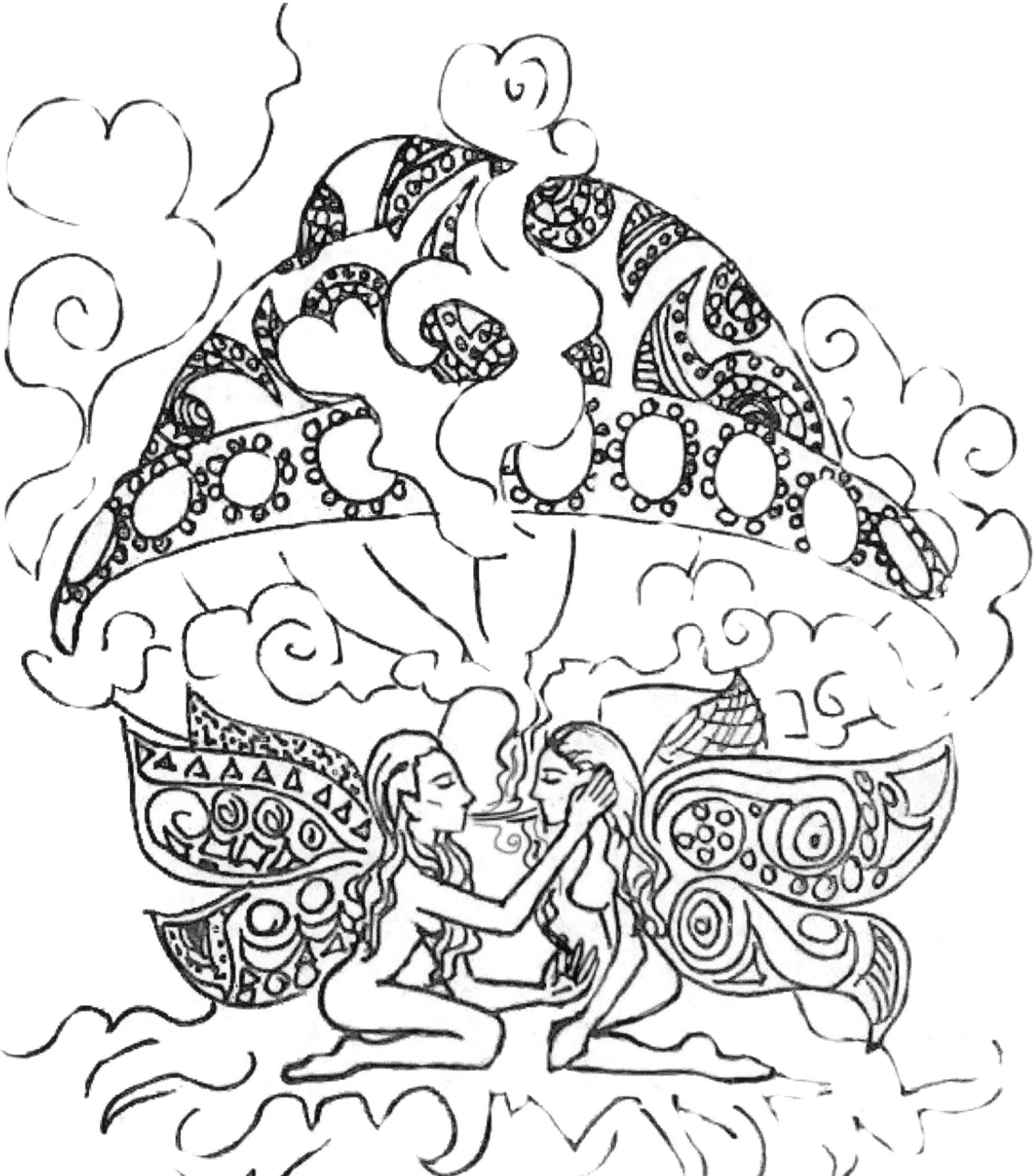

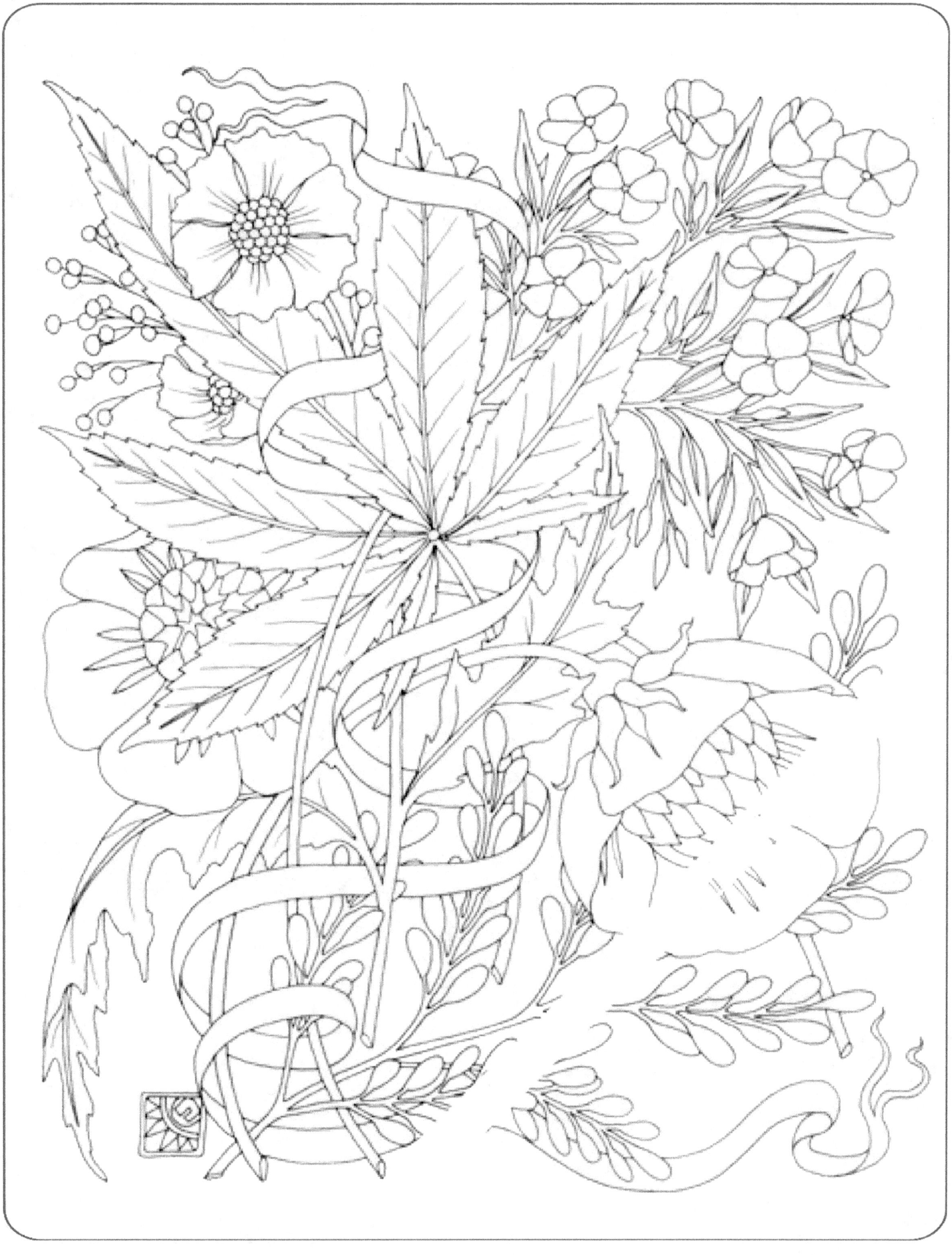

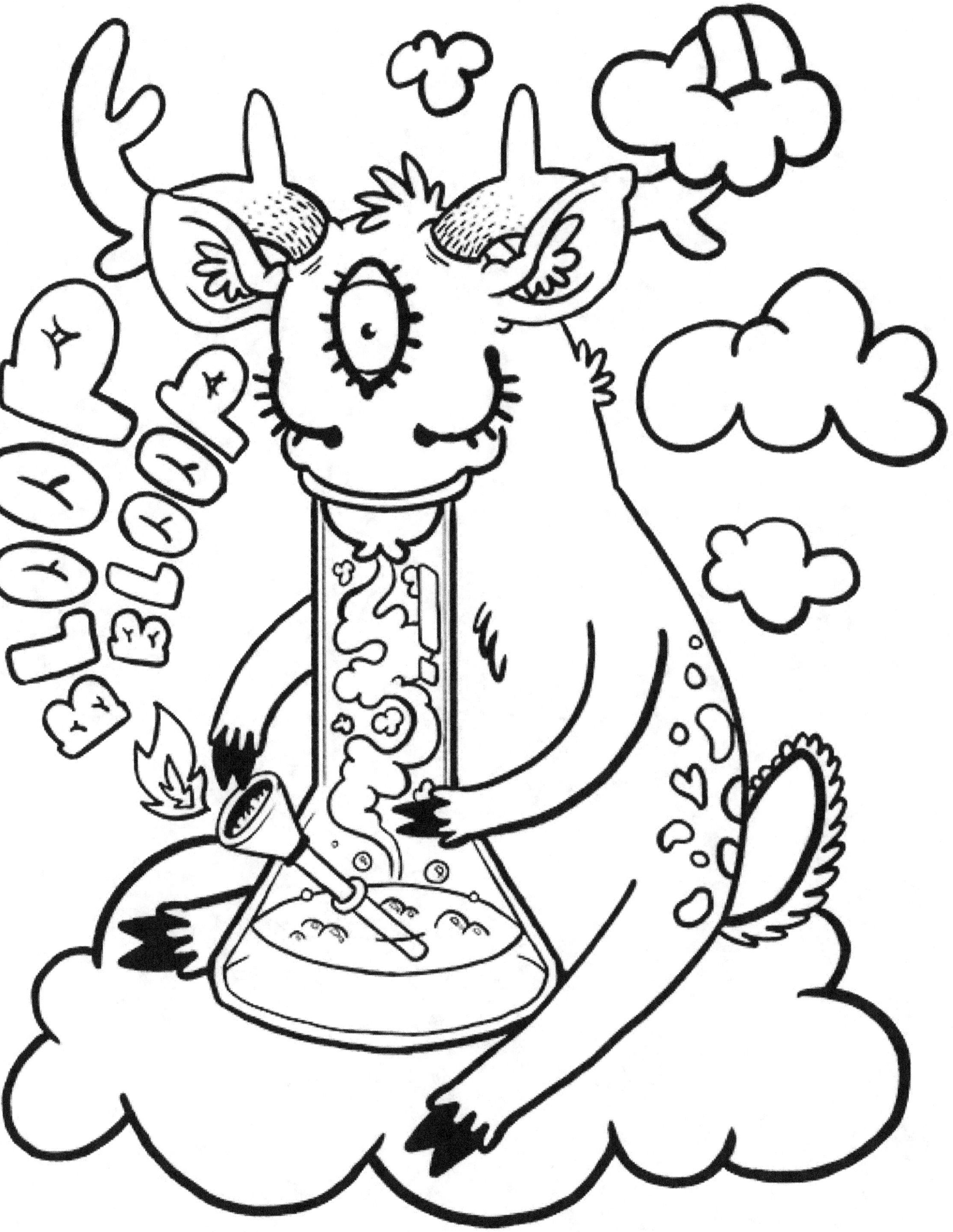
BLOOP
BLOOP

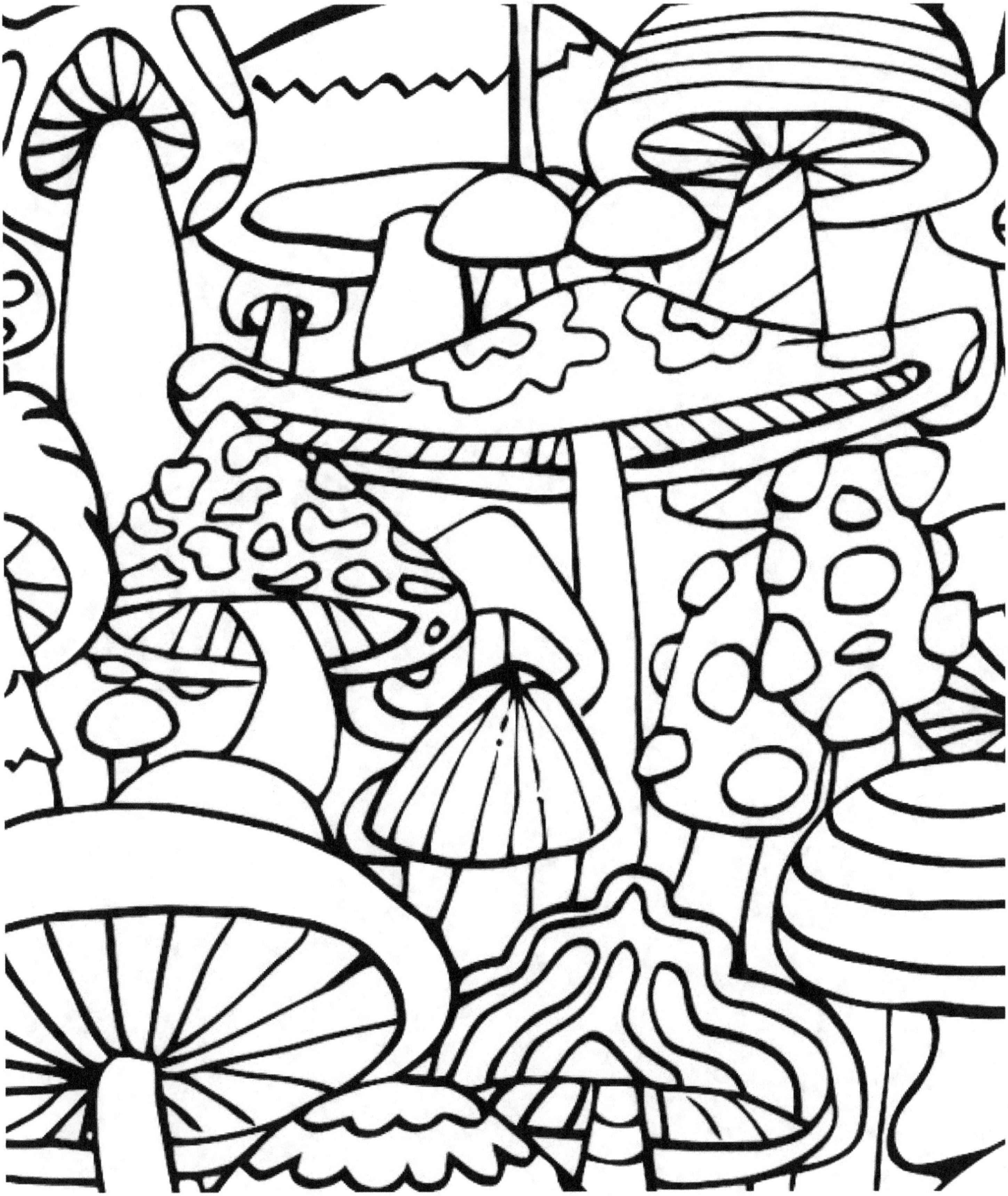

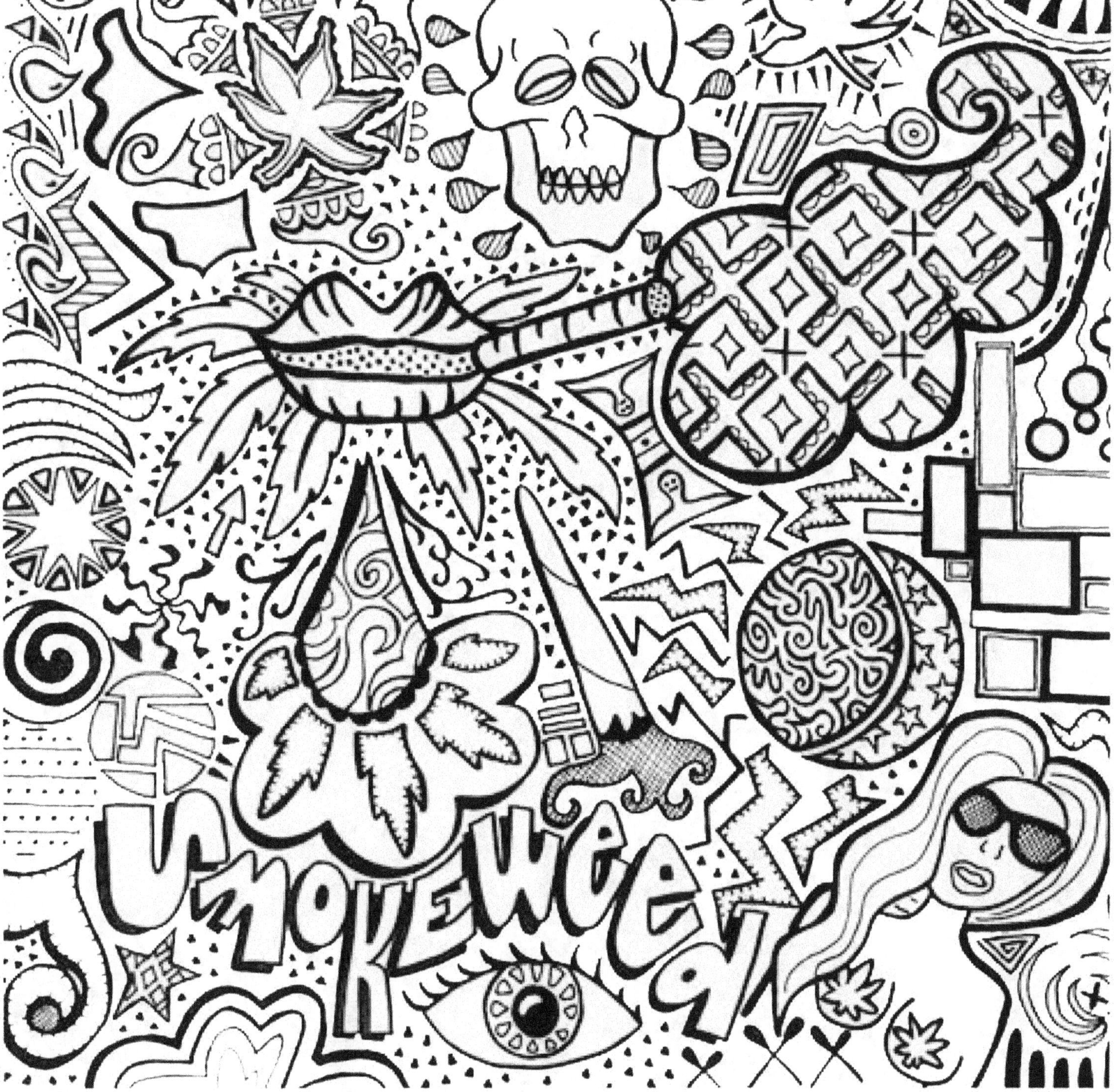

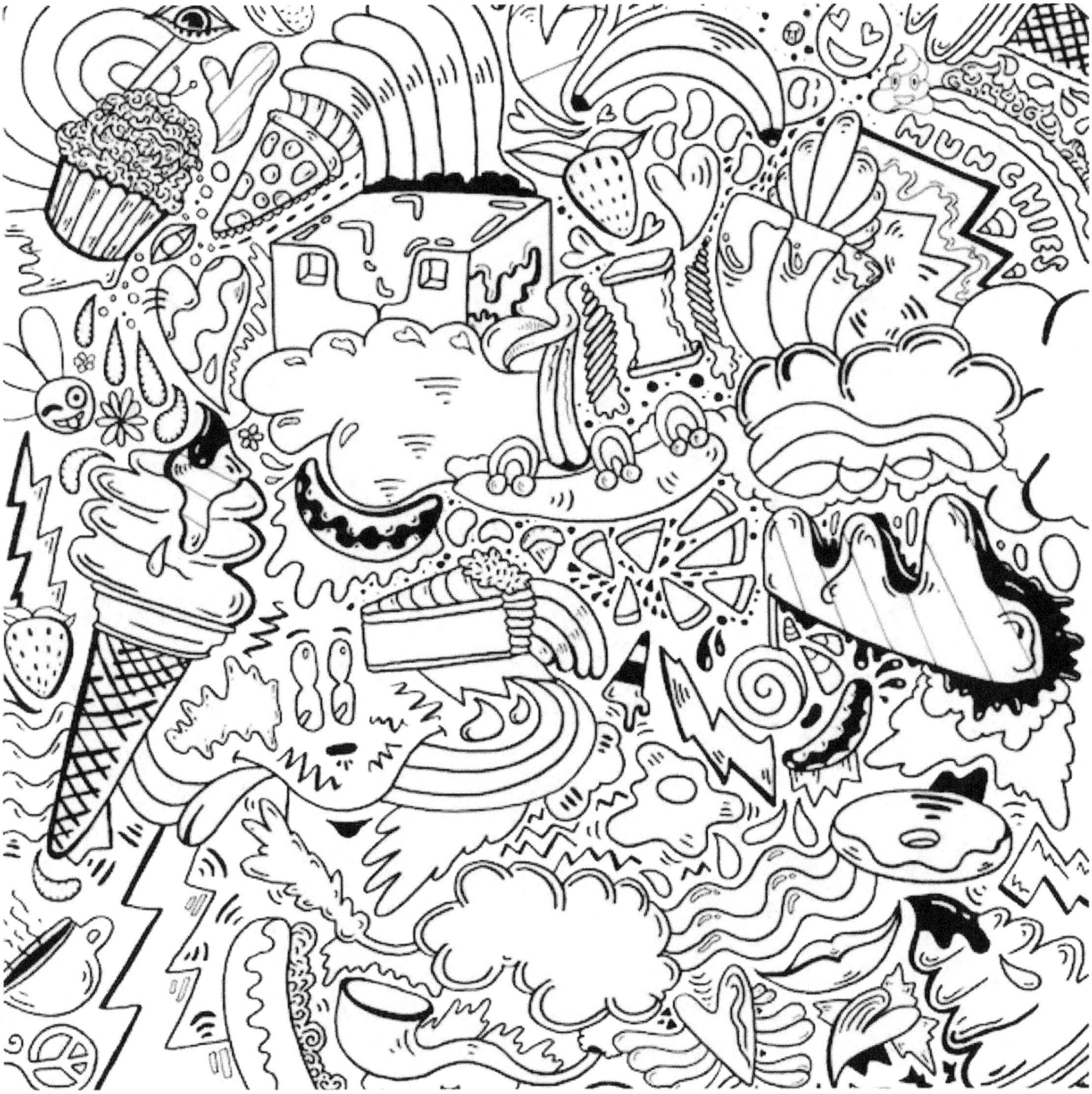
MUNCHIES

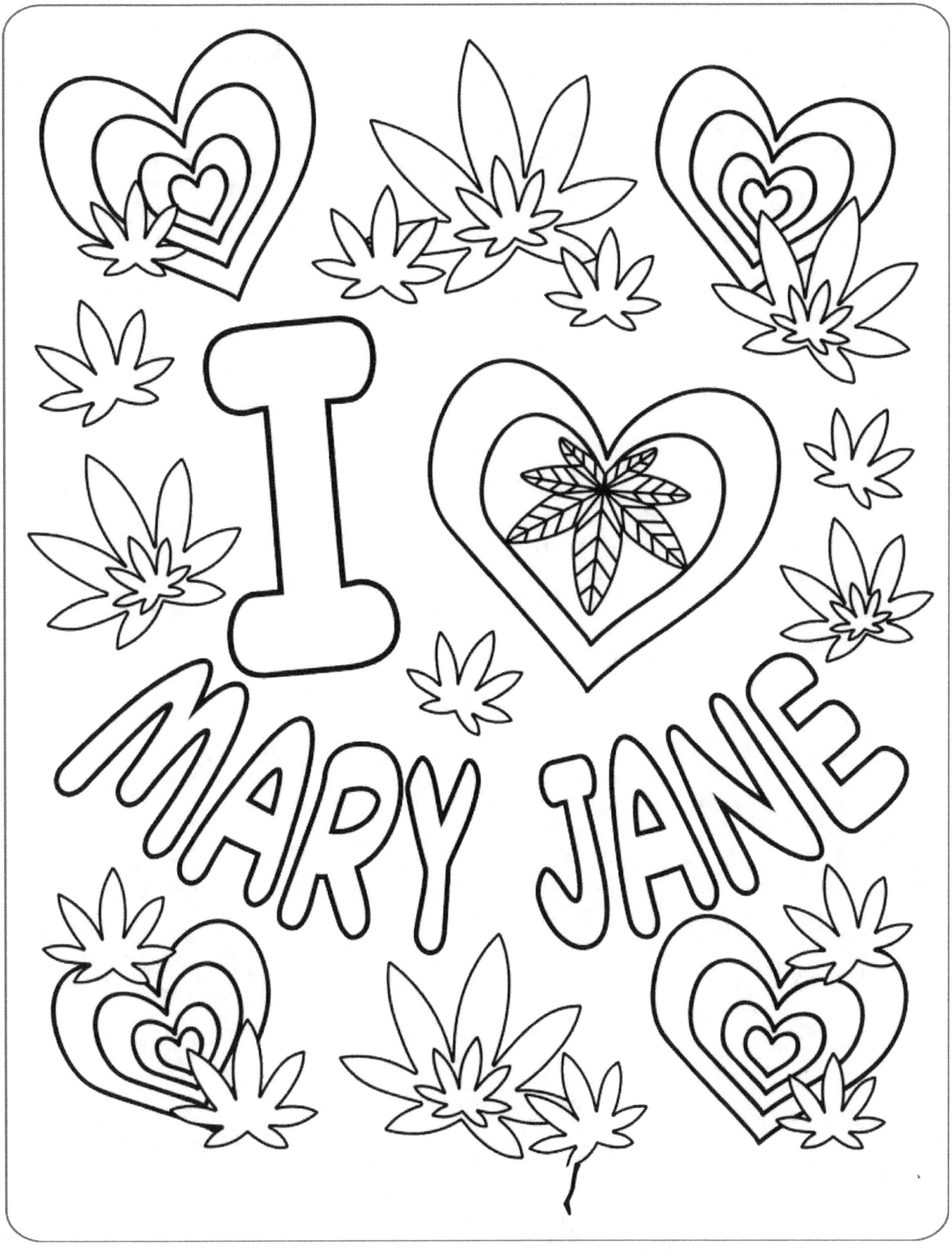
I
MARY JANE

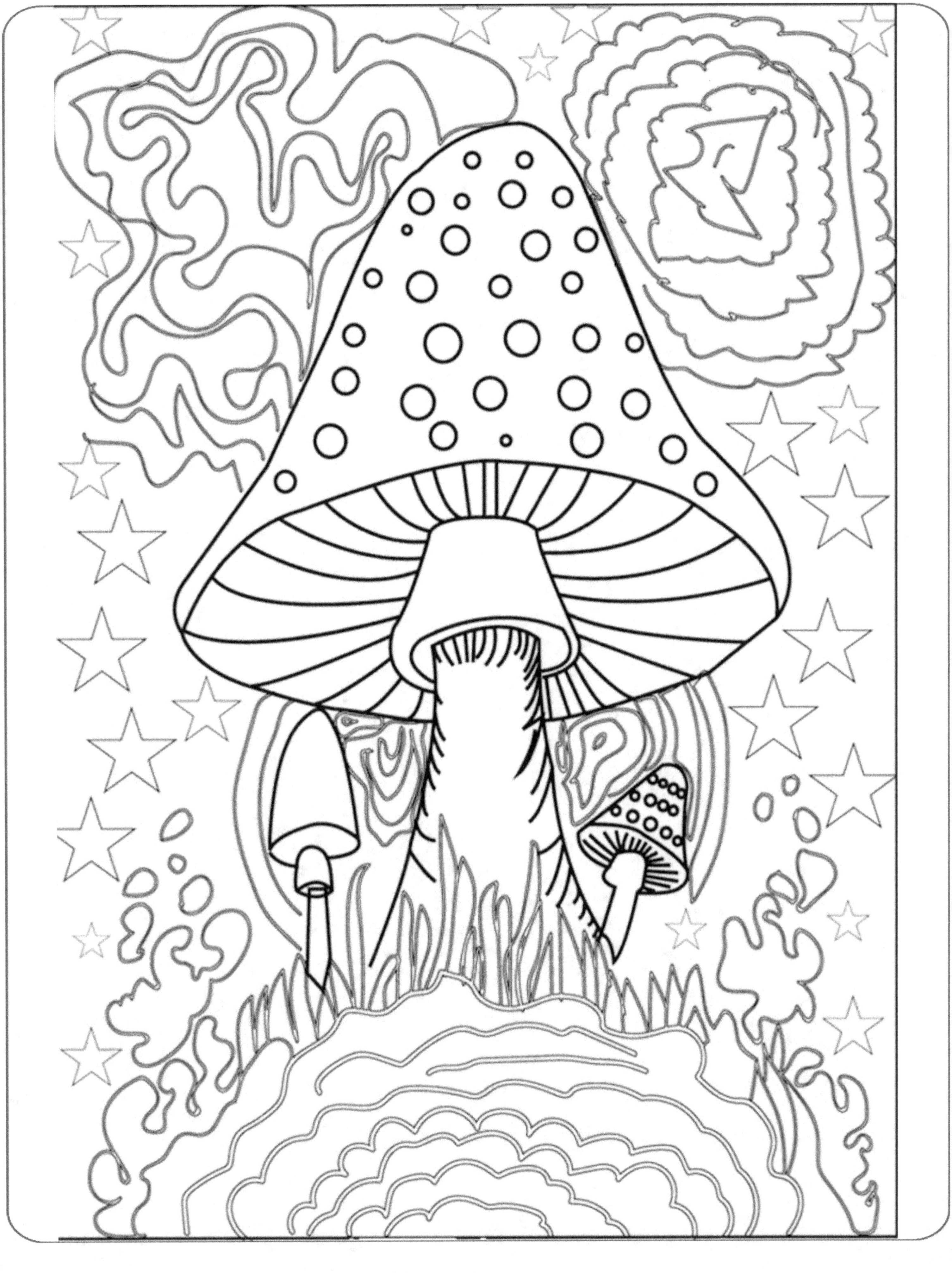

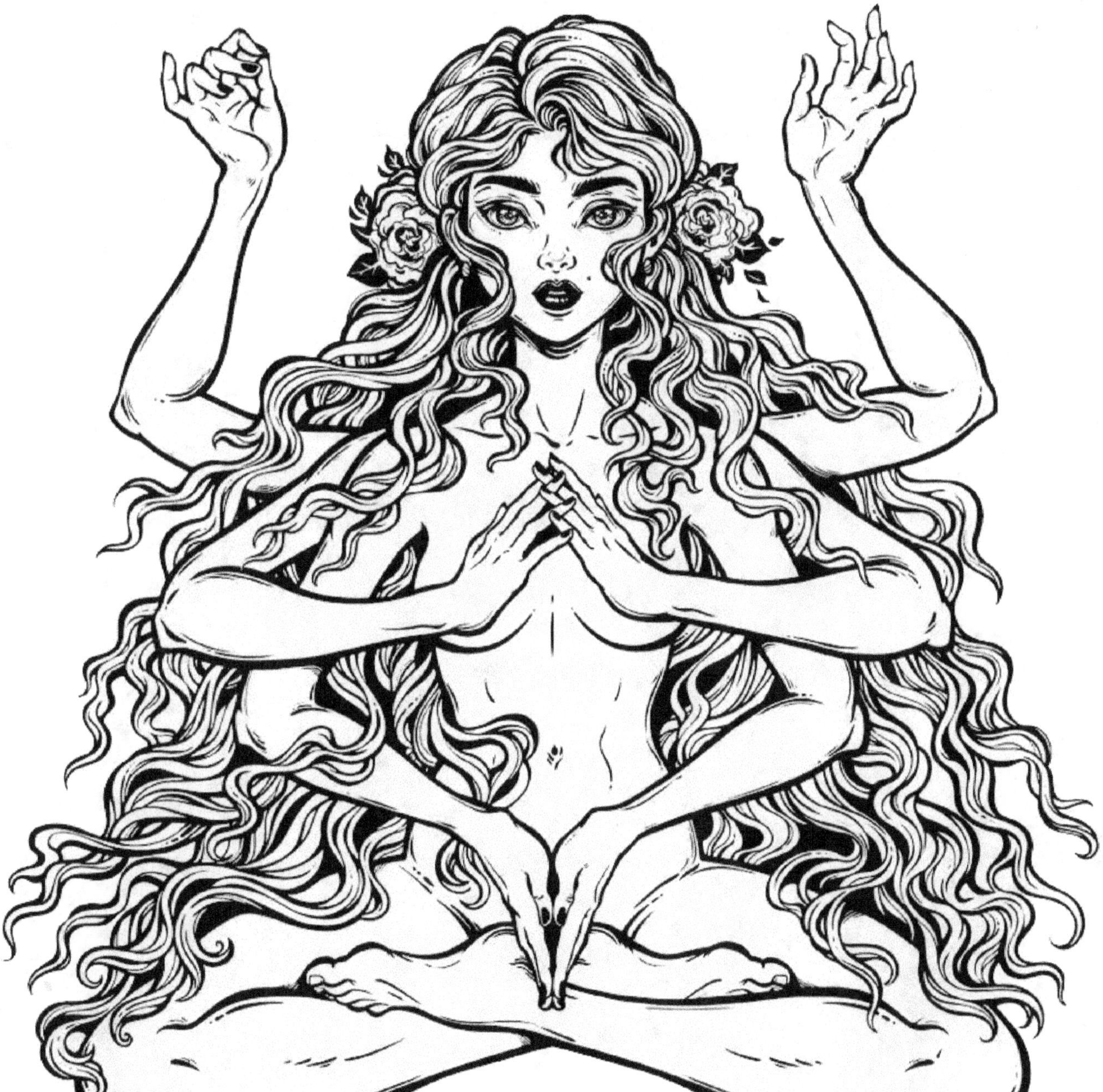

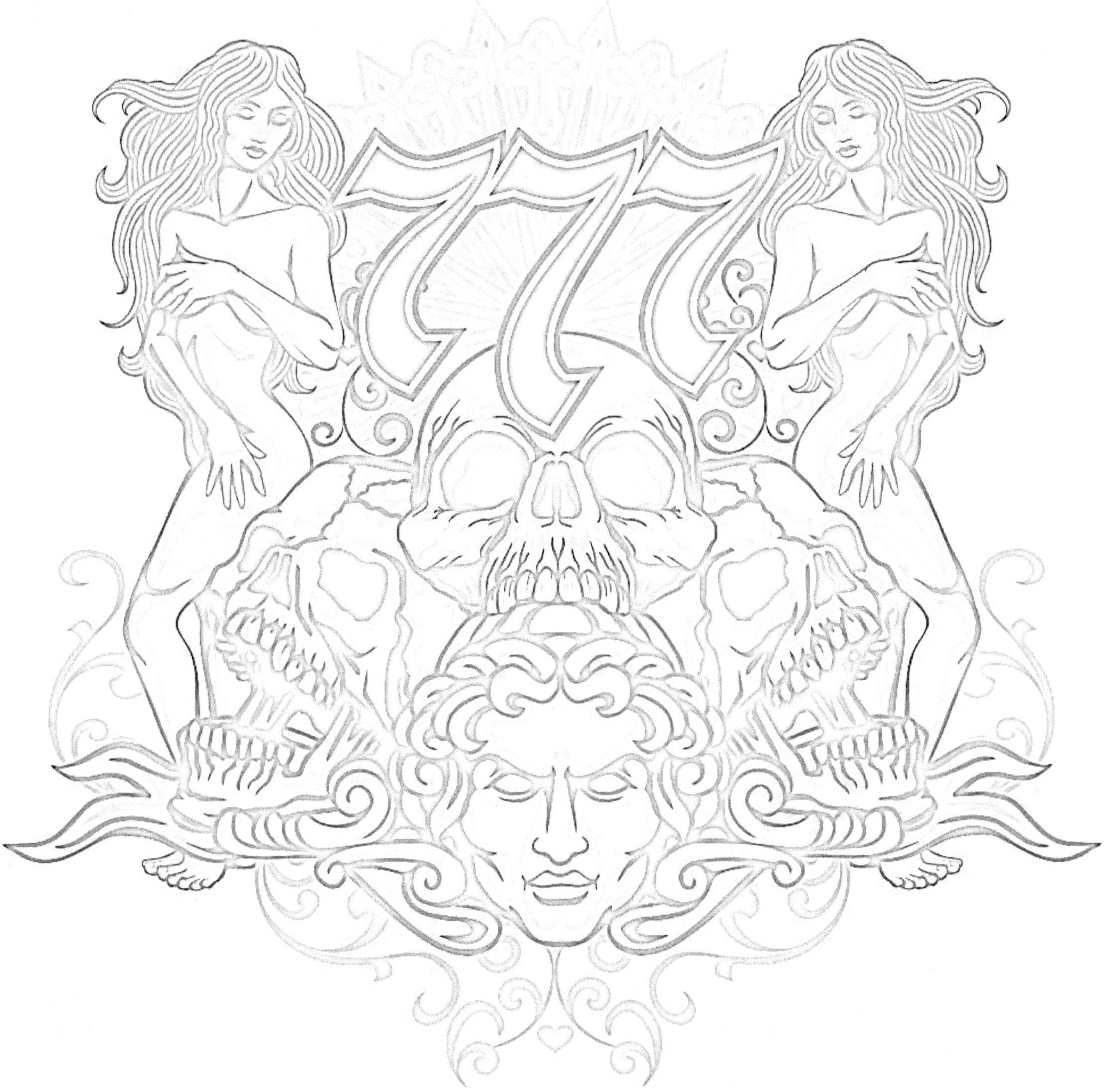

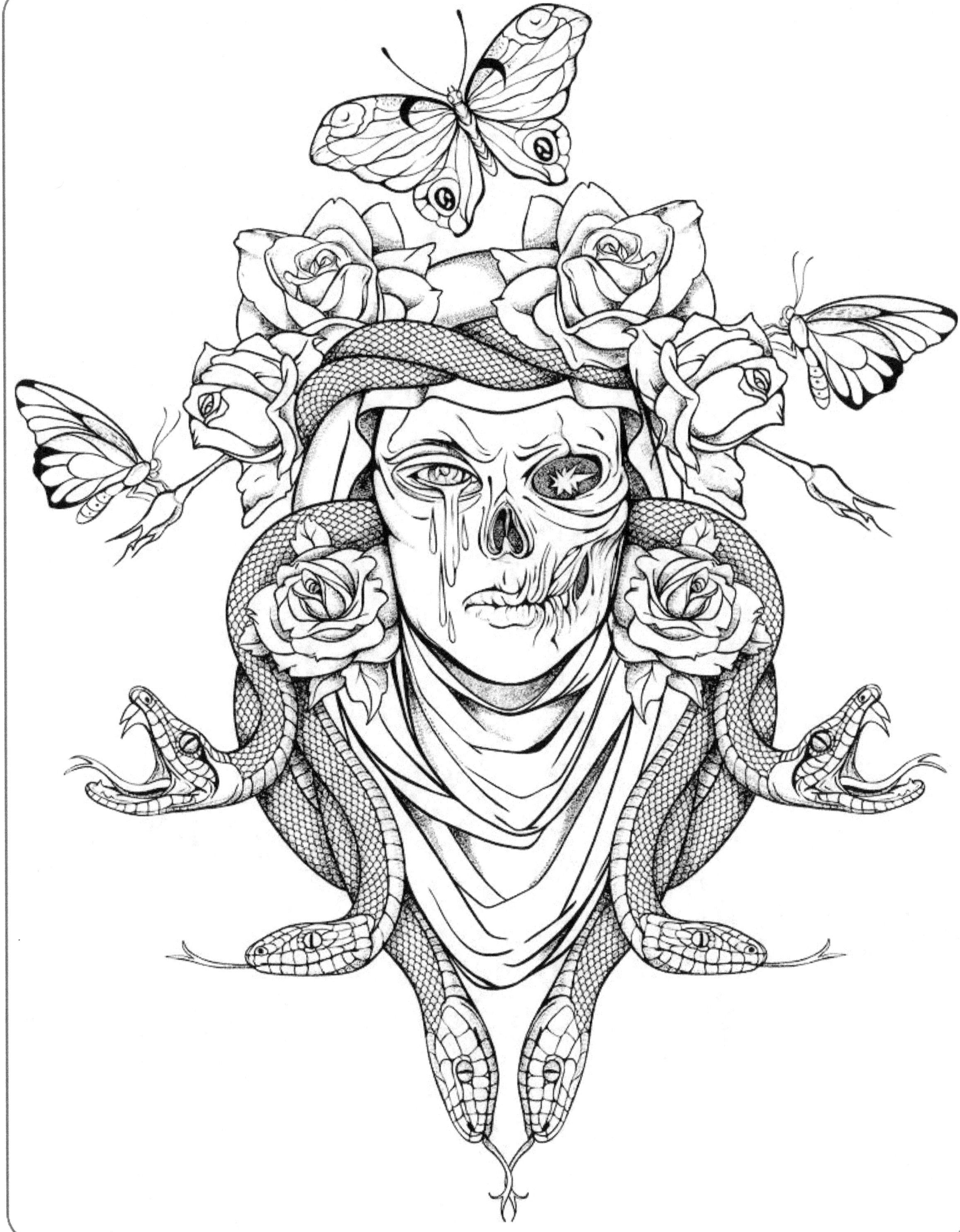

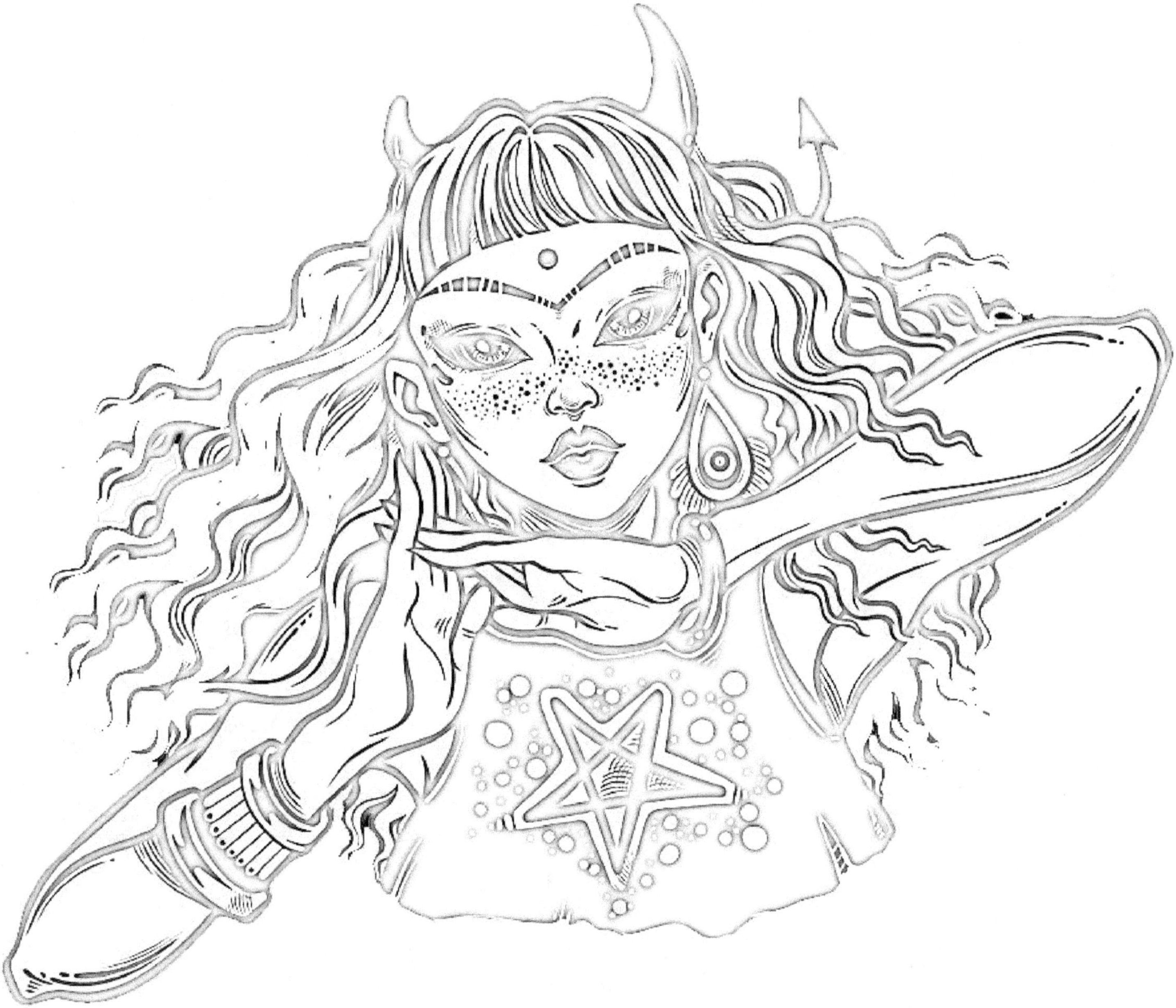

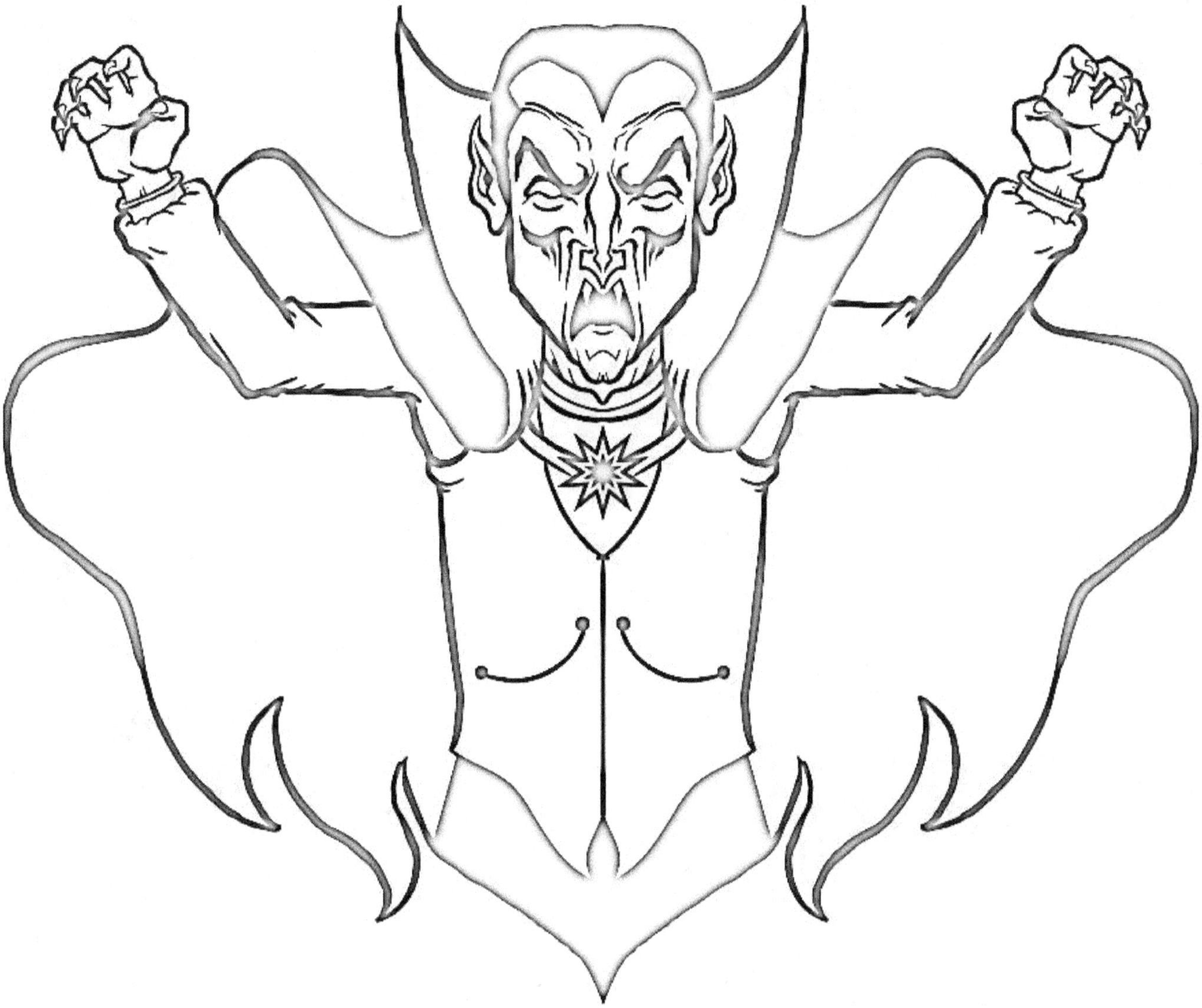

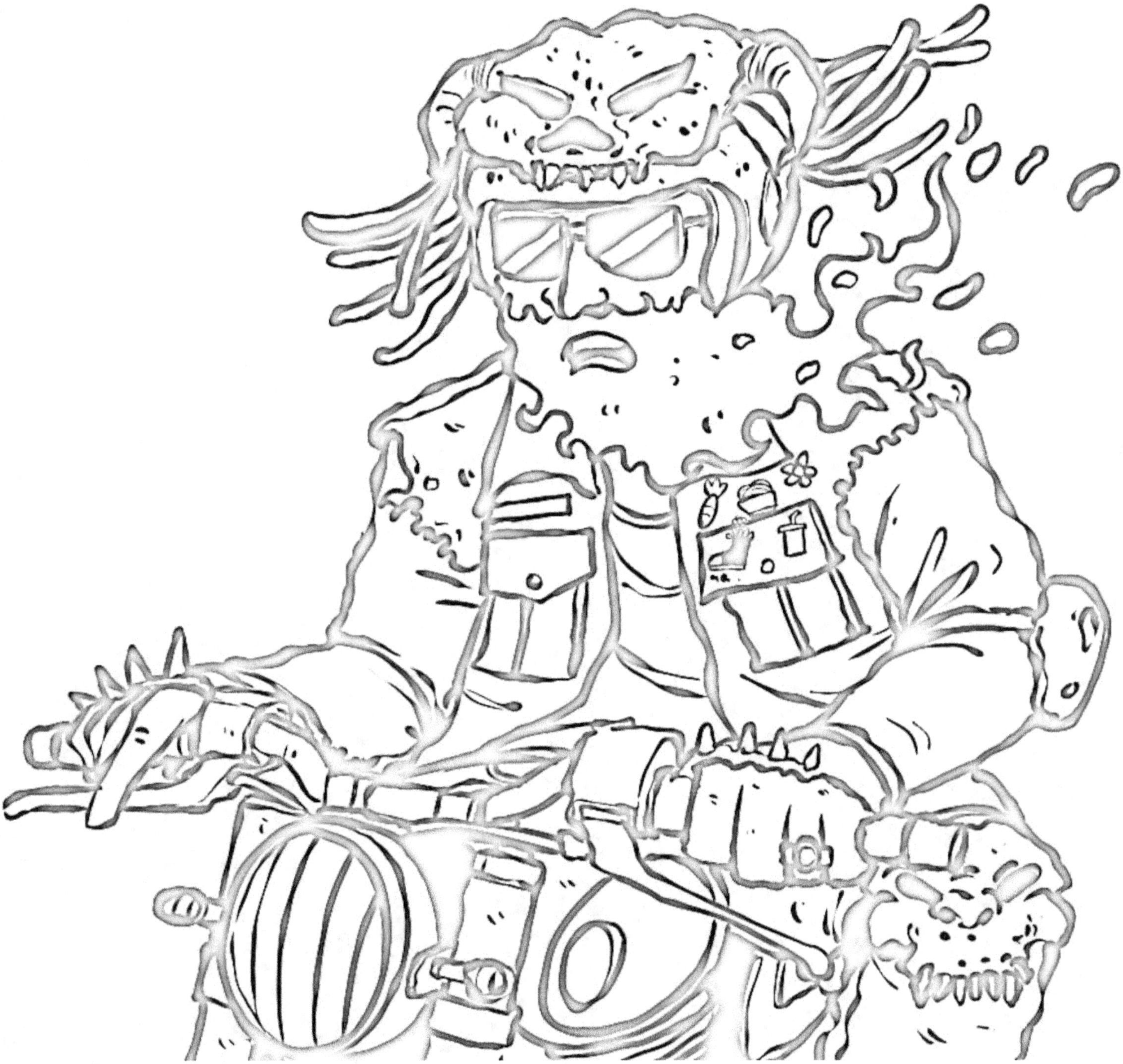

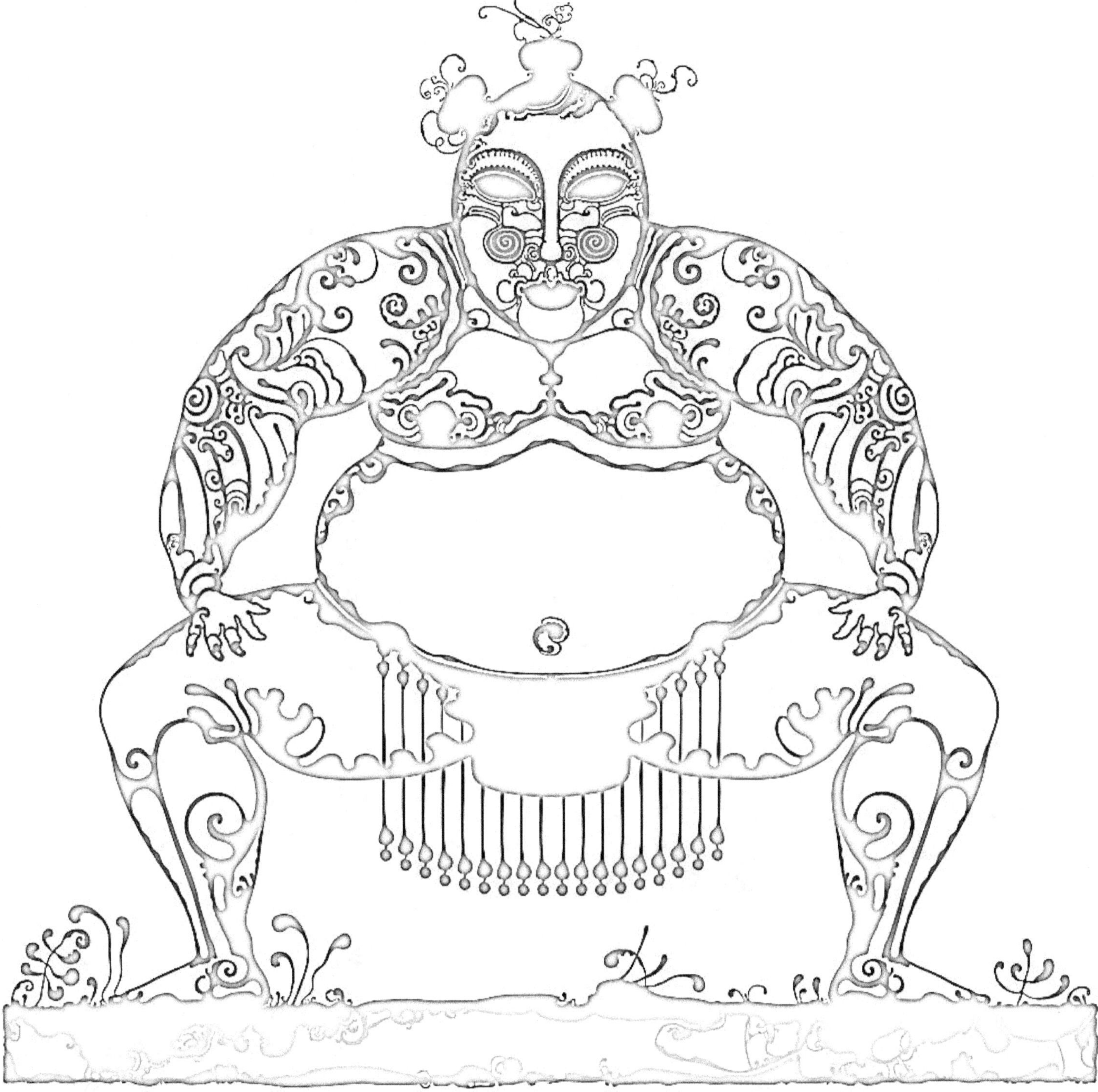

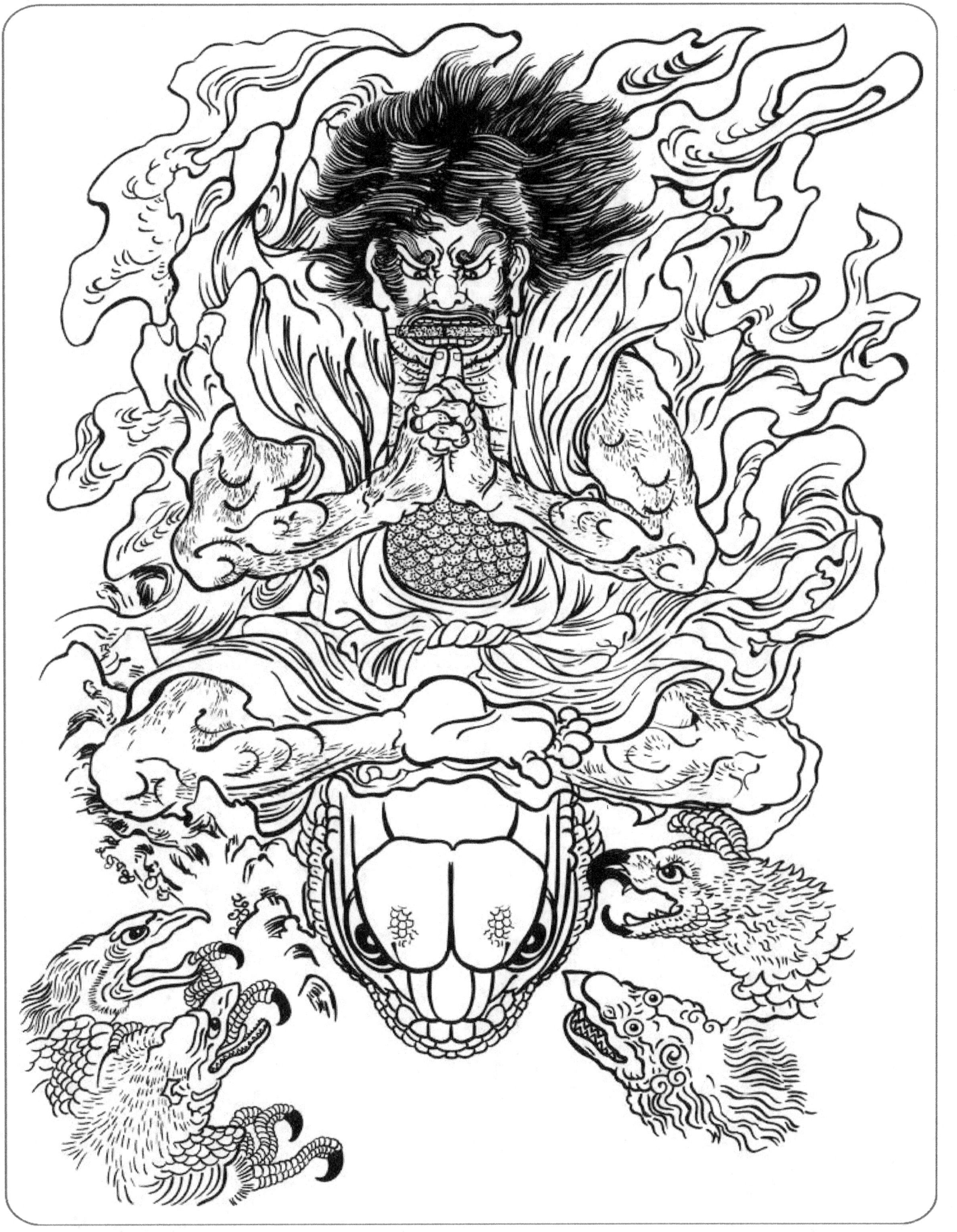

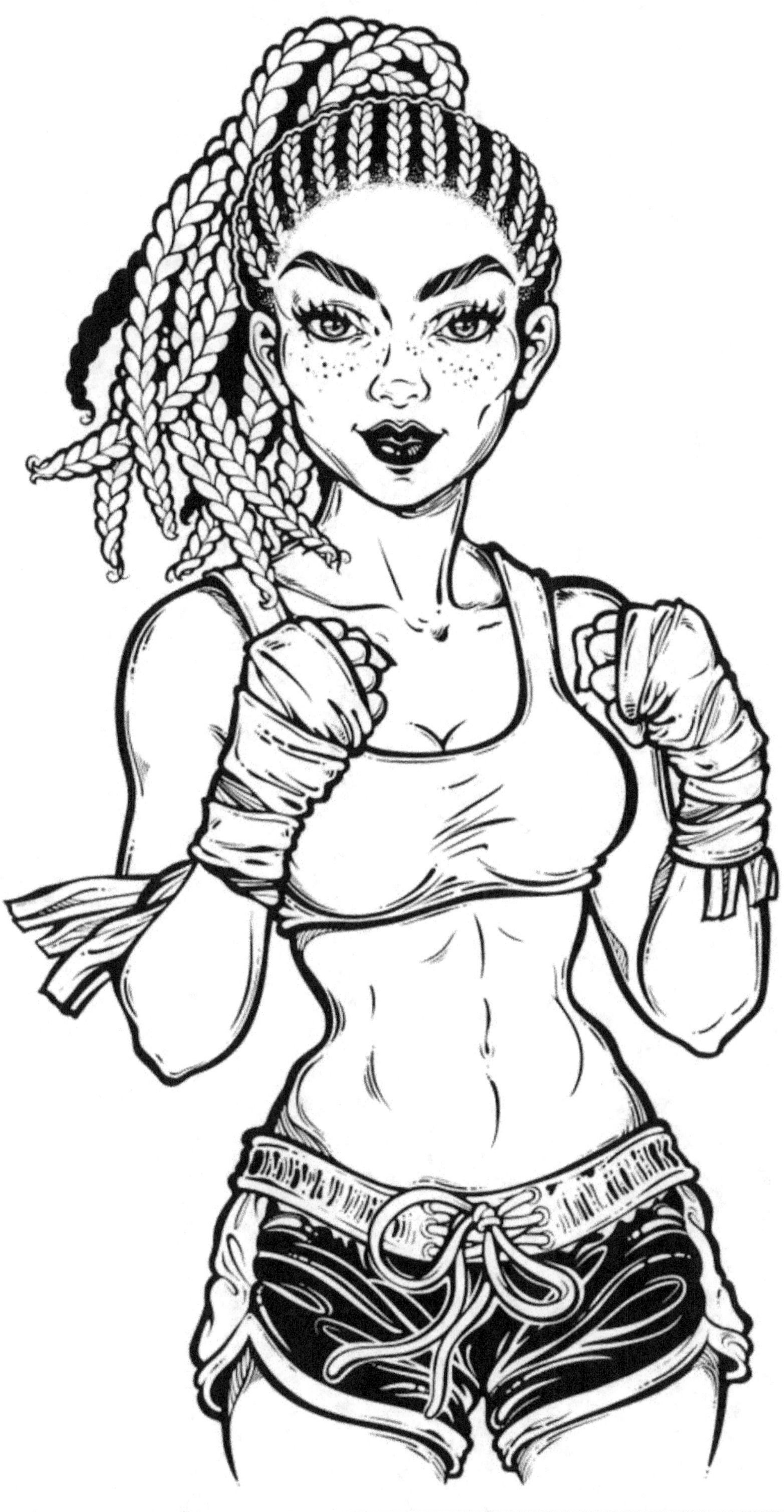

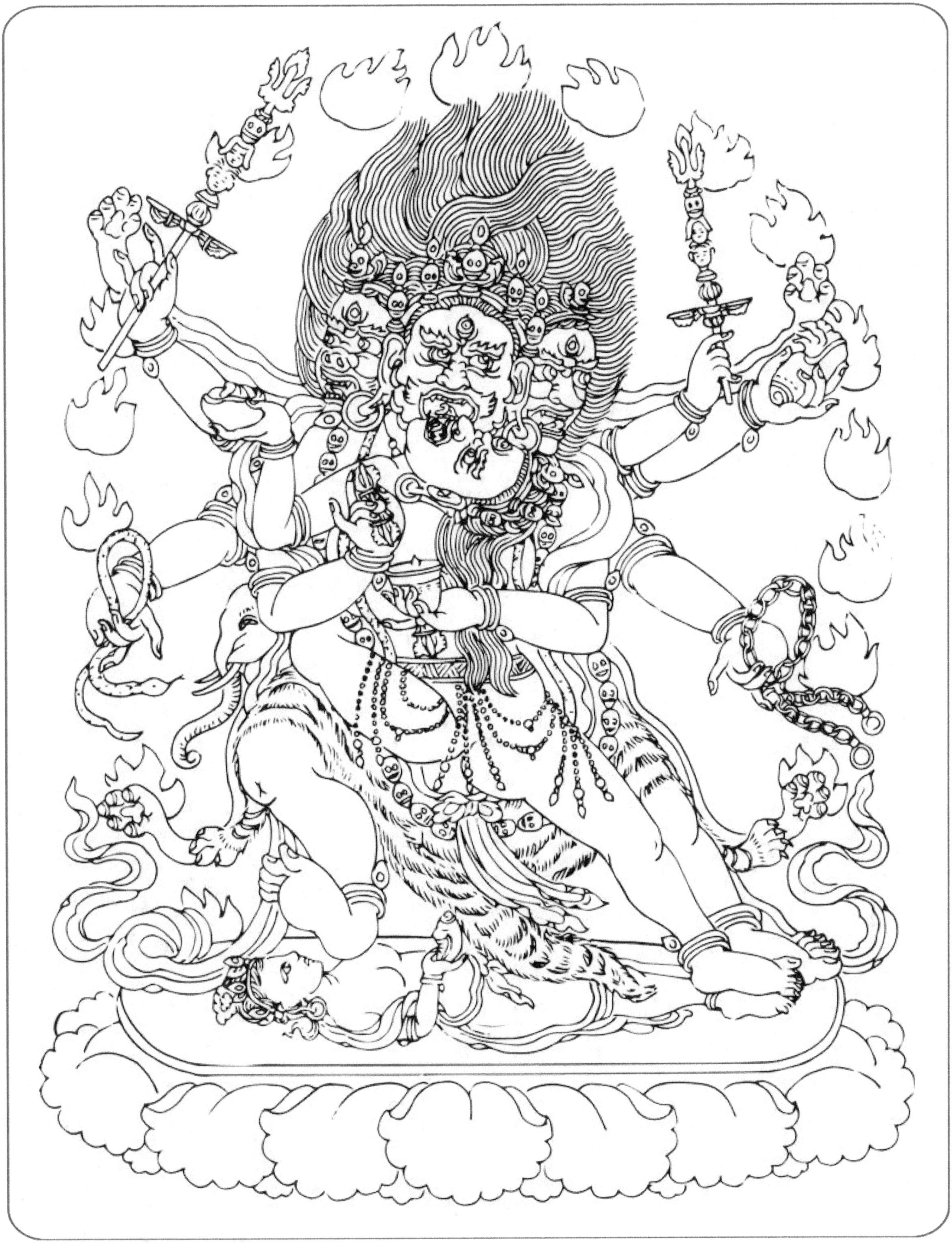

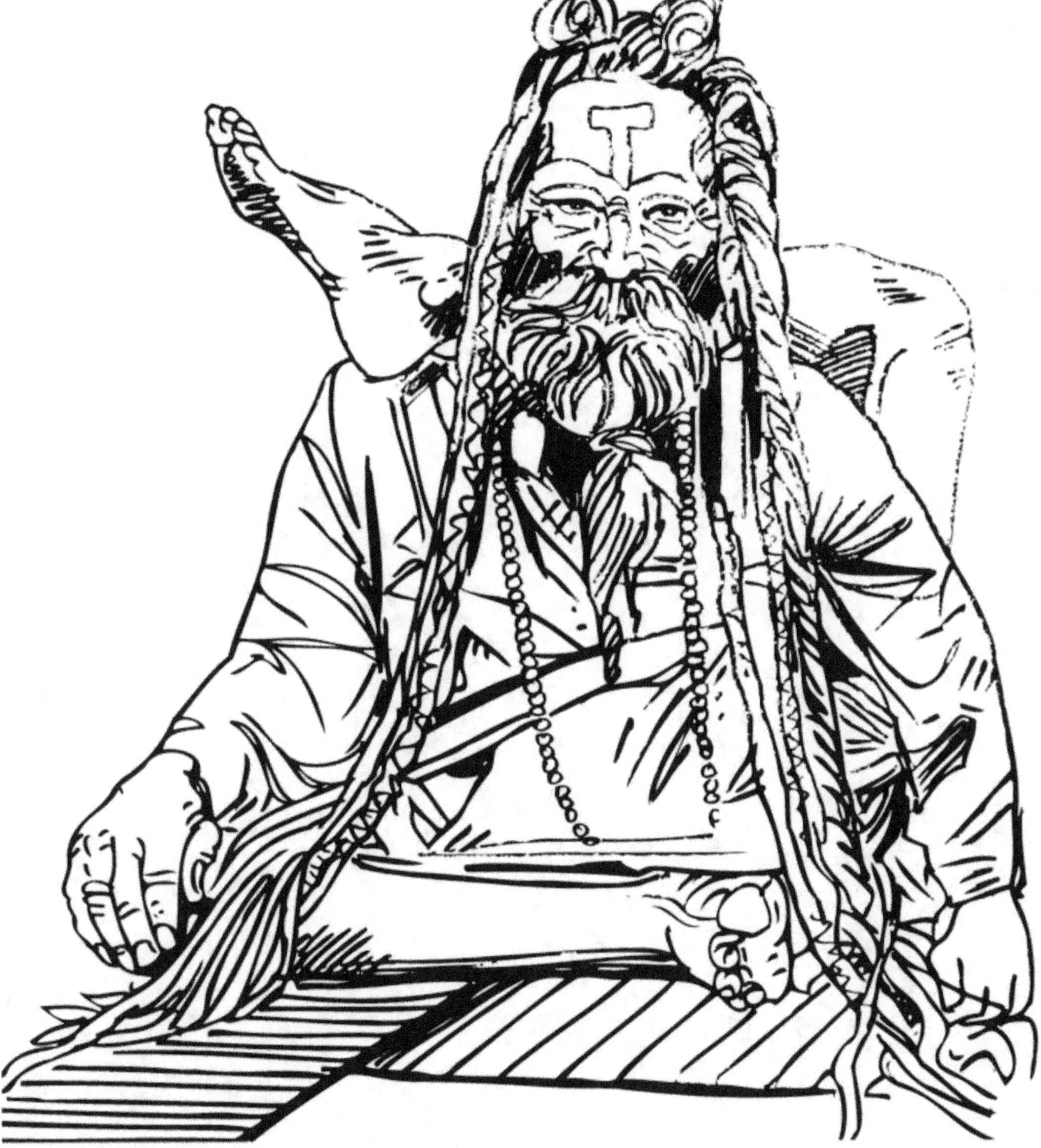

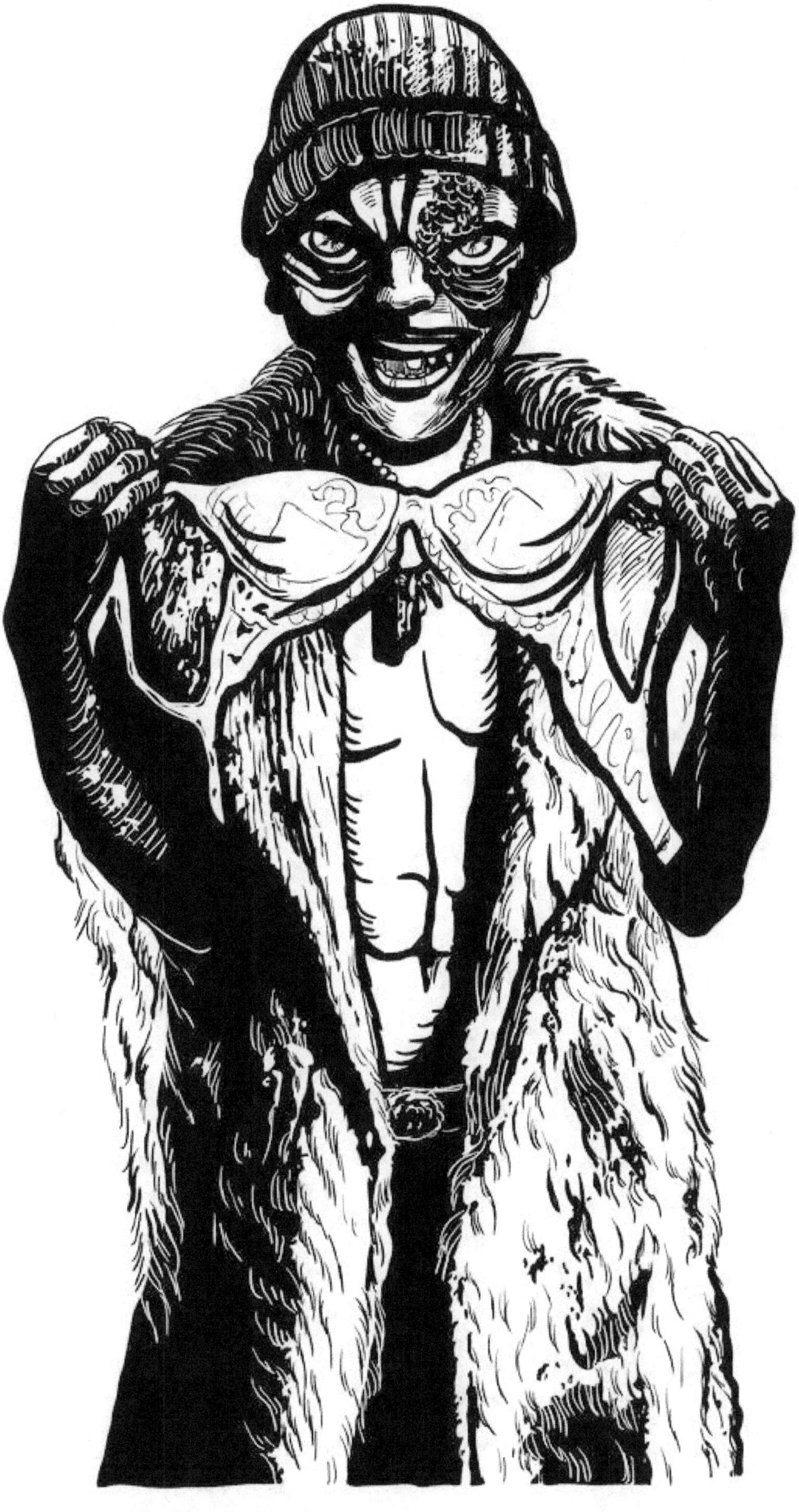

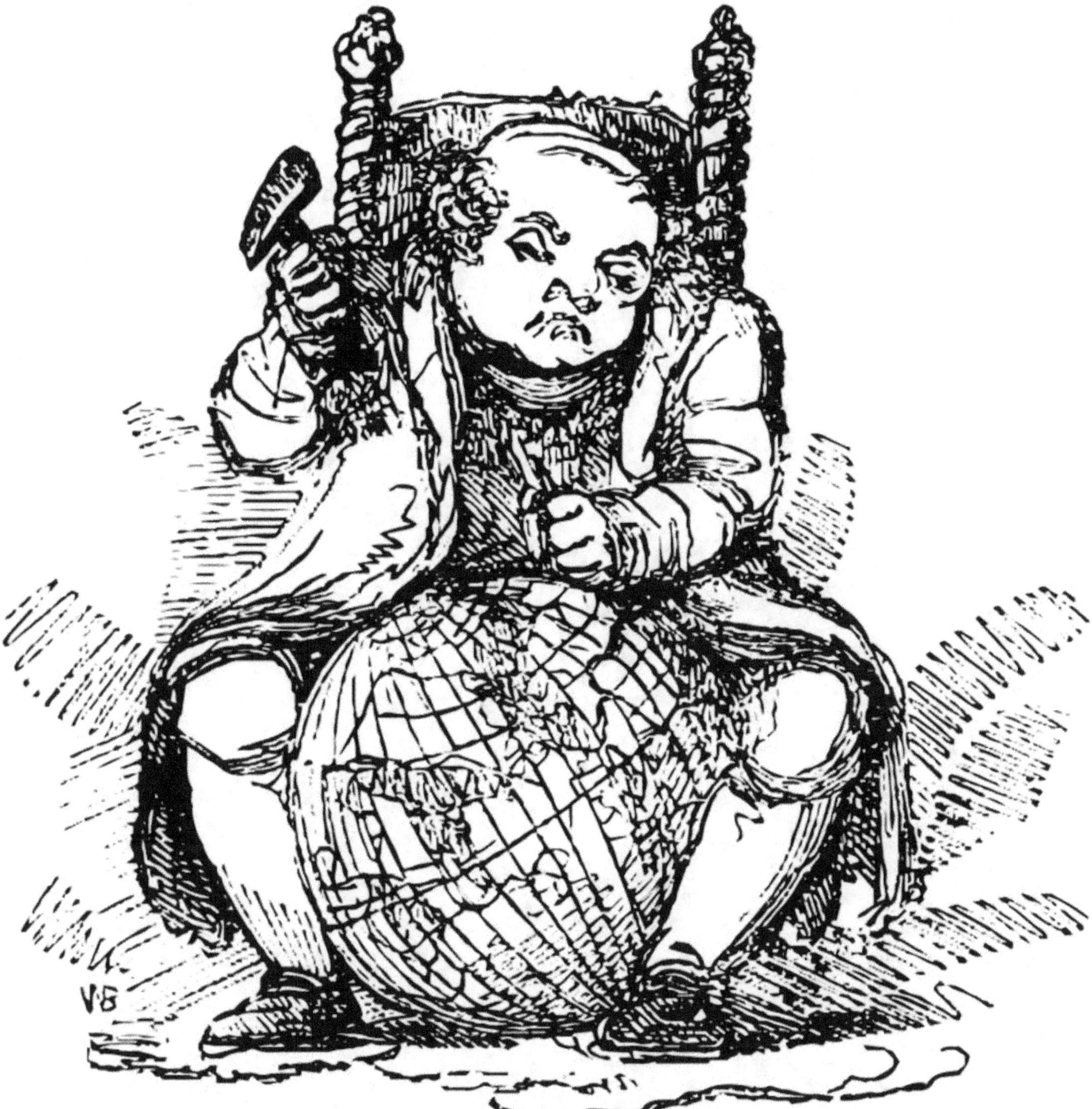

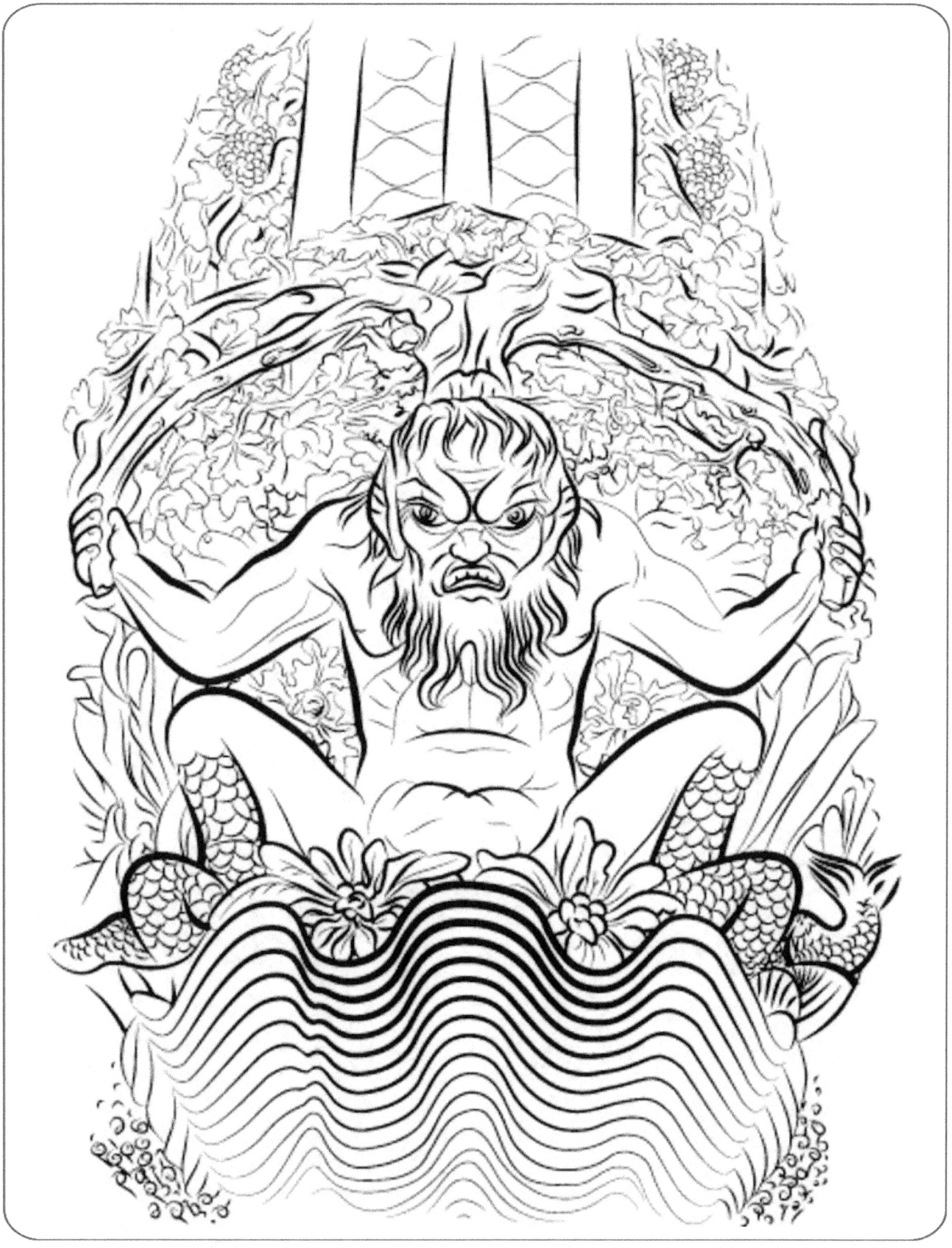

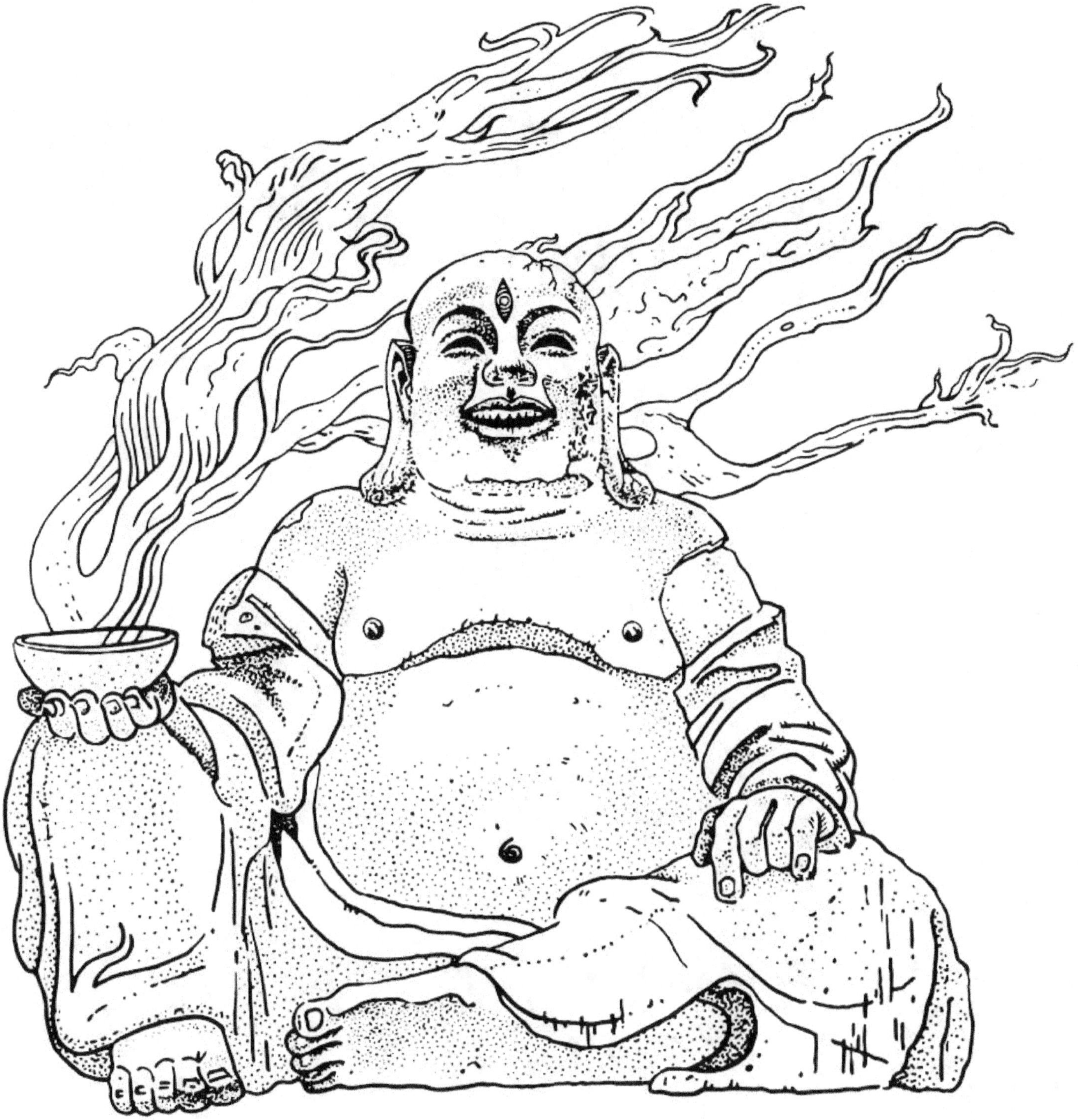

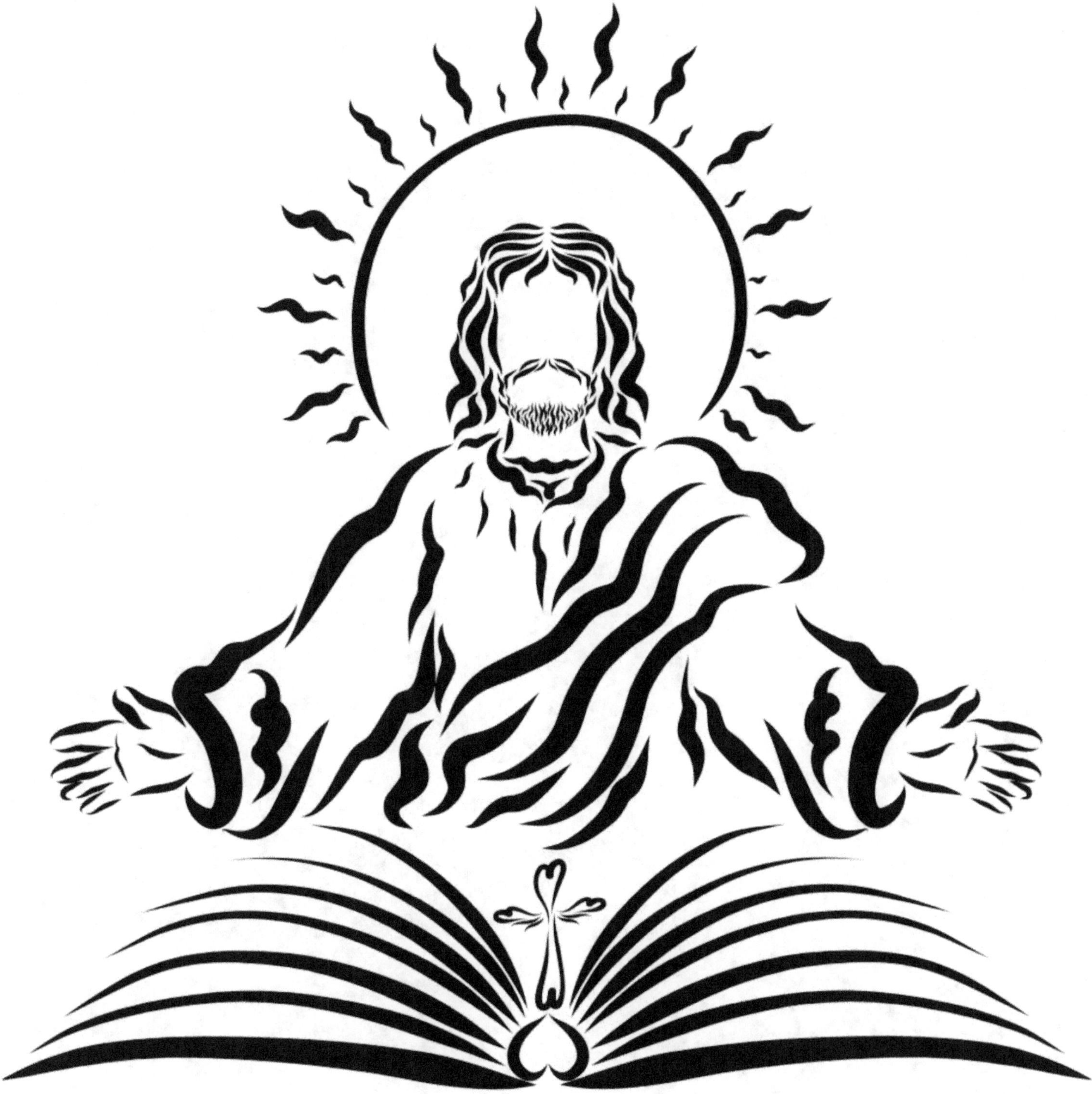

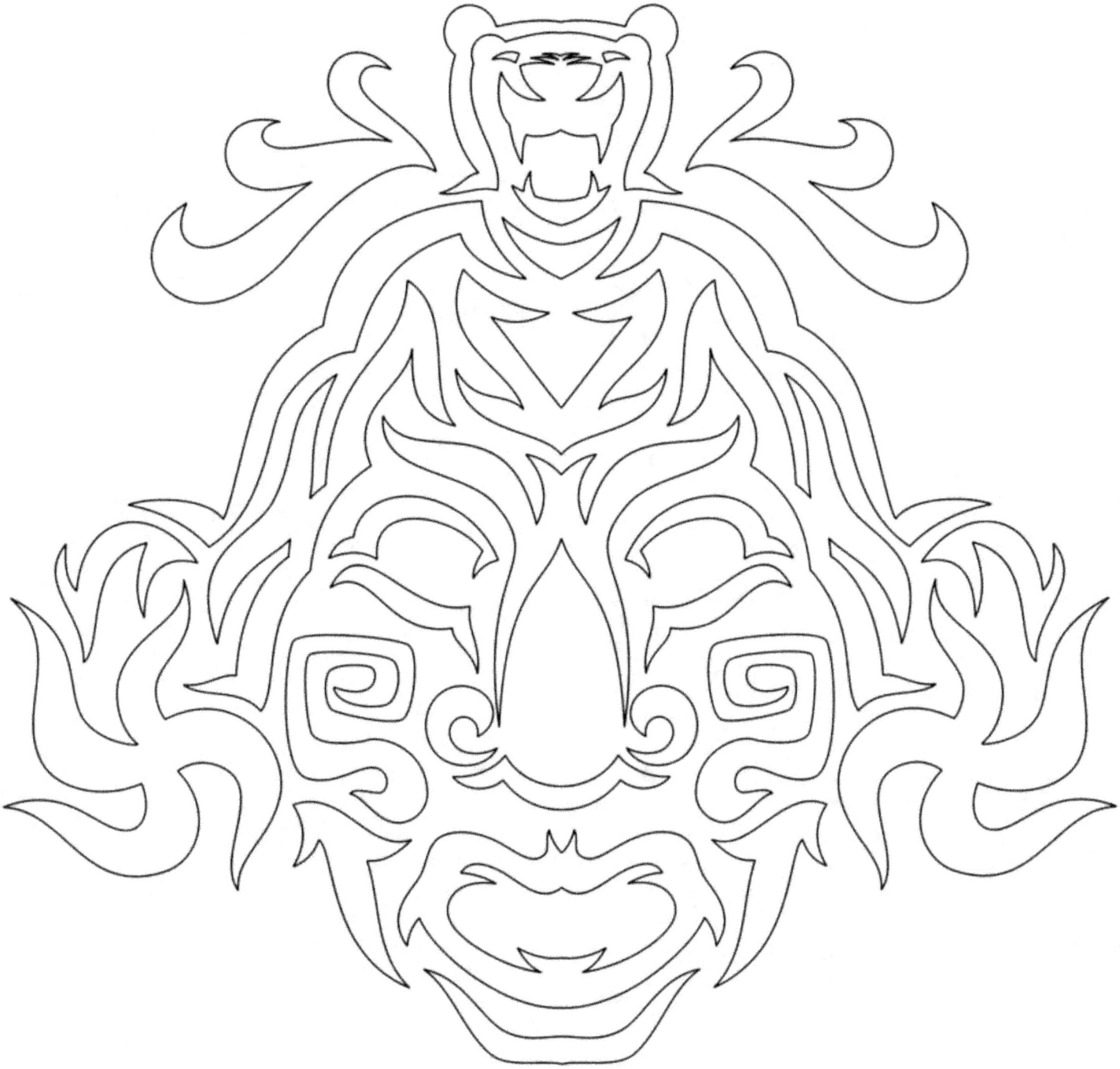

www.ingramcontent.com/pod-product-compliance
Lightning Source LLC
Chambersburg PA
CBHW081528220526
45467CB00010B/3091
* 9 7 9 8 6 8 5 5 0 2 1 0 0 *